PRAISE FROM EIG
THE ASTONISHING PC

From this point forward, this b⟨ ⟩d friends I keep on my nightstand and pack during long travel journeys. I encourage every educator to give yourself the gift of *The Astonishing Power of Storytelling*—it will have a profound impact on your personal and professional journey.

Stephanie Hirsh, Executive Director, Learning Forward; Oxford, OH

You will never find a more insightful book on the nature and power of storytelling as leadership. This book will stir your emotions, inform you, and inspire you to rethink how you lead. It will then guide you to become a better storyteller by helping you "shift perceptions, invite learning, inspire action, and seek a new desired state" in your local context. A unique and inspiring leadership book.

Michael Fullan, Professor Emeritus, Ontario Institute for Studies in Education—University of Toronto; Toronto, Canada

Garmston captures the science *and the magic* of stories as essential tools for leading, collaborating, communicating, and connecting, showing how and why leading through story is vital in our complex world. This book is a must read for education leaders of all kinds—principals, central office leaders, facilitators, and all who want to support the growth of others in powerful ways.

Ellie Drago-Severson, Professor of Education Leadership & Adult Learning and Leadership, Teachers College, Columbia University; New York, NY

This book has comprehensiveness, careful structure, and graceful writing. Garmston didn't just pick a topic and write a book. This wisdom piece has been a lifetime in the making. It is really quite something.

Jon Saphier, Founder and President, Research for Better Teaching; Acton, MA

We hear stories every day. But we don't necessarily tell—or retell—stories well. Every leader needs to reach people, their hearts and minds, and Garmston's new book speaks to the power of storytelling for just this purpose. A surprising read, I now see stories differently, as sparks for human transformation.

Wenny Kusuma, United Nations, Women Country Representative; Kathmandu, Nepal

In this book, Garmston—a mesmerizing storyteller himself—brings an age-old tradition to life with useful guides for crafting good stories and using them in our work and daily lives.

David Chojnacki, Executive Director Emeritus, Near East South Asia Council of Overseas Schools; Athens, Greece

It has been said if you want to change the culture, change the story. Garmston has been a premier professional development trainer and practitioner for over thirty years. This book will provide background knowledge and great practical tips on the use of stories as a teaching strategy.

William Sommers, Bricoleur, Leadership Coach, & Author; Austin, TX

For eons, storytelling has linked one generation of humanity to another and Robert J. Garmston does us all a great favor by reminding us that story is the conduit of human experience. Those who lead, present, and consult will find this book an enduring friend for influencing and communicating to a variety of audiences, especially in one's own voice.

James L. Roussin, Executive Director of Generative Learning, Strategic Change Consultant/ Leadership Coach; Stillwater, MN

With rare insights, Garmston offers many pathways into the practice of storytelling, most powerfully by showing how metaphors are basic structures for making stories meaningful, heartfelt, and enlightening across diverse cultures.

David Hyerle, Author of *Pathways to Thinking Schools* (2014); Lyme, NH

Guided by his rich life experience in helping educators embrace meaningful learning and development in schools, Garmston has brought us another gem! He offers the why, what, and how for using this most effective means of inspiring change in individuals and organizations.

Sally Alturki, Co-founder of Dhahran Ahliyya Schools and the Educational Book House; Dhahran, Saudi Arabia

In *The Astonishing Power of Storytelling* Garmston confirms with brain science and sound research what we all know intuitively—stories have the power to both persuade and inspire. What's more, the book is chock-full of practical tips and approaches to plan and deliver stories with intention and aplomb. Bob has gifted all of us an excellent "how to" manual to make our stories sing!

Joelle Basnight, High School Principal, American International School; Chennai, India

Inspiring . . . this book will add to your leadership capacity and help shape you into a storyteller to transform your skills as a professional.

Kelly Armitage, Elementary School Principal, International School; Bangkok, Thailand

Garmston has taught me most of what I know about presenting and this book is a wonderful addition to my repertoire. The scaffolds and rich examples provide models for my own storytelling that I can now harvest from my life experiences. I am already crafting an introductory story for my next workshop.

Lucy Fisher, Manager Emeritus, Learning Education Department Educational, Consultant; Tasmania, Australia

Robert J. Garmston has touched upon who teachers naturally are. Storytellers. Throughout *The Astonishing Power of Storytelling* Garmston provides evidence that validates the power of telling stories, and offers tools to enhance the innate instincts of a teacher. This book will nurture abilities that some are not aware they possess. After all, what is teaching but a way to inspire students to search for knowledge? What better way to set the stage than to "Tell a Story"?

Karen Tribble, Elementary School Teacher; Fairfield, CA

One of the most important facets to effective change leadership is the ability to engage and create meaning. In *The Astonishing Power of Storytelling* Garmston draws the connection between an engaging story and the ability to stimulate positive change.

Gregory A. Hedger, Director, The International School;
Yangon, Myanmar

Al-Hakawati in Arabic is a person who narrates the old stories transferring values and traditions across generations and inspiring the listeners. In this sense Garmston's *Astonishing Power of Storytelling* is a transcultural book; one can help you use storytelling in your profession with easy-to-follow-and-use tools and strategies.

Jihad Dwaidar, Literacy Coach, International Programs
School; Khobar, Saudi Arabia

Garmston's latest book, *Astonishing Power of Storytelling* is a welcome resource which strategizes the use of storytelling for leaders at all levels. The skills he offers through storytelling can help present sometimes bland information with personal and internalizing effectiveness. For leaders who seek to achieve lasting change, this book makes impressive sense!

David B. Cloud, Alaska Administrator
Coaching Project; Homer, AK

This book has helped me to understand and experience how storytelling is an essential element for anyone who presents, lectures, or conducts workshops. *The Astonishing Power of Storytelling* encouraged me to use storytelling as a strategy to hold the students' attention and better achieve my instructional goals of shifting their perceptions, while encouraging learning and action. As I prepared talking points on working with resistant teachers for my class on supervisory practice, stories from personal experience came to mind. While sharing a story with my students about a teacher I was working with, I demonstrated the body language (crossed arms and legs) he displayed during the post-observation conference. We then explored what was being said by this body language and strategies for how to respond effectively. The results were amazing. Not only were the students intrigued, the story also enabled me to engage them in meaningful discussion with productive results. This book will continue to be my guide as I prepare for future classes and presentations.

Marcia Knoll, Professor, Educational Administration, Hunter College; New York, NY

Great storytelling feels almost magical. It creates natural connections between speakers and listeners that are personal, meaningful, and authentic. We all remember the stories that captivate us, inspire us, and open our minds to new ideas. Storytelling is at the heart of good teaching and this guidebook promises to teach all of us to become splendid storytellers. I can't wait to share it with my teacher education students.

Aixa Perez-Prado, Professor of Education, Florida International University; Miami, FL

I remember gathering around my mom and watching her stories light up the room as I listened. Her stories had a big impact on who I am today. This book is a perfect guide to discover your own personal story and suggests ways for why and how you can use your story to make a memorable impact on others.

Servet Altan, International Educator and Educational Researcher, Bilkent University; Ankara, Turkey

Garmston provides astonishing examples of the power of storytelling. Through storytelling, he shows that wit and wisdom can be companions on the journey to gain knowledge and insight.

Gary Whitely, Leadership Consultant; Kenai, AK

THE
ASTONISHING
POWER
OF
STORYTELLING

THE

ASTONISHING POWER

OF

STORYTELLING

*Leading, Teaching, and
Transforming in a New Way*

ROBERT J. GARMSTON
Illustrations by Dede Tisone

CORWIN
A SAGE Publishing Company

CORWIN
A SAGE Publishing Company

FOR INFORMATION:

Corwin
A SAGE Company
2455 Teller Road
Thousand Oaks, California 91320
(800) 233-9936
www.corwin.com

SAGE Publications Ltd.
1 Oliver's Yard
55 City Road
London EC1Y 1SP
United Kingdom

SAGE Publications India Pvt. Ltd.
B 1/I 1 Mohan Cooperative Industrial Area
Mathura Road, New Delhi 110 044
India

SAGE Publications Asia-Pacific Pte. Ltd.
3 Church Street
#10-04 Samsung Hub
Singapore 049483

Printed in the United States of America

Library of Congress Cataloging-in-Publication Data

Names: Garmston, Robert J., author.

Title: The astonishing power of storytelling : leading, teaching, and transforming in a new way / Robert J. Garmston ; illustrations by Dede Tisone.

Description: Thousand Oaks, California : Corwin, 2018. | Includes bibliographical references and index.

Identifiers: LCCN 2018015390 | ISBN 9781506386393 (pbk. : alk. paper)

Subjects: LCSH: Communication in education. | Educational leadership. | Public speaking. | Persuasion (Rhetoric)

Classification: LCC LB1033.5 .G37 2018 | DDC 372.67/7—dc23 LC record available at https://lccn.loc.gov/2018015390

This book is printed on acid-free paper.

Publisher: Arnis Burvikovs
Development Editor: Desirée Bartlett
Editorial Assistant: Eliza Erickson
Production Editor: Andrew Olson
Copy Editor: Deanna Noga
Typesetter: C&M Digitals (P) Ltd.
Proofreader: Sarah J. Duffy
Indexer: Amy Murphy
Cover Designer: Gail Buschman
Marketing Manager: Nicole Franks

FSC
www.fsc.org
MIX
Paper from responsible sources
FSC® C005010

18 19 20 21 22 10 9 8 7 6 5 4 3 2 1

CONTENTS

PREFACE

Public figures without storytelling chops are probably 50% less effective than they could be. Leaders who get promoted to increasingly higher levels of leadership, says John Hennessy, Stanford University's 10th president, are those who tell compelling and inspirational stories. He sees this as an essential skill set for bringing people together and unifying them to a single vision. Such leadership skills don't happen on their own, he says; they must be developed (Malone, 2018).

A leader's job is to persuade, and stories persuade more effectively than reports, studies, statistics, or PowerPoint presentations. Savvy leaders know this and incorporate stories in their efforts to influence others. Neuroscientists know that stories influence listeners at even subterranean levels. Chemicals released in the listener's brain launch a neurological ballet that directs attention beyond simple language processing to centers of experience that evoke empathy, a desire to help, and motivation to behave as did the main character in whatever story was told. This book presents new understandings about the mechanisms of persuasive stories, describes how to design (or recognize) them, and reveals the stagecraft involved in motivational storytelling.

Those whose responsibility is to guide others—leaders such as teachers, principals, mentor teachers, curriculum specialists, professors, superintendents, and presenters, no matter how currently successful in teaching or influencing others—will find their abilities to persuade enhanced by a storytelling repertoire. This book addresses the what, the why, and the how of storytelling and explains how to do this in oral presentations.

Stories saved me in my first teaching assignment. As an intern I had not completed teacher-training courses and subsequently greeted my first class of 42 fifth graders with lots of love but no teaching skills. At the time the fifth-grade curriculum in California featured the western movement in U.S. history. Without skills, and without much knowledge, I chanced upon Irving Stone's book *Men to Match My Mountains* (1956), a compelling history of California, Nevada, Colorado, and Arizona from the 1840s to the 1880s. Stone used stories to convey circumstances of bravery, vision, perseverance, economics, politics, creativity, and simple dumb luck. I borrowed shamelessly from what I read and captivated those 10-year-olds.

Much later in my career, presenting to educators, I learned about storytelling to adults from John Grinder. I clearly remember the first time I gave myself permission to tell stories to groups of my peers. At that time I was as terrified of storytelling as some people are of public speaking. I was afraid that telling a story wasn't a good use of the audience's time and that it would take away from the important concepts to be communicated. Furthermore, new to presentation work, I was often distracted and worried by inactive or scowling participants, which rendered me less effective.

Because of a seminar with Grinder, a master at weaving narratives through his teaching, I decided to try his approach myself. I found my fears had been dead wrong. The moment I began to tell stories, my own as well as those I had heard from others, audience members perked up and began to attend with laser intensity and I started to have more fun. So did audiences and groups I led in my roles as principal, director of instruction, acting superintendent, and professor. And, I suspect, they carried away more in their hearts and their minds. Additionally, I found stories to be more persuasive than suggestions when working one-on-one.

This book is for those new to using stories in their work, as well as those with existing comfort and repertoire. To begin the journey of using story or advance to new levels of effectiveness, all that is necessary is to try. So, to make this book worth your while, pick a setting, choose or make up a story, and test it with an individual or small group. The odds are great that your experience will be like mine—an attentive reception. It's hard to fail, because good stories are irresistible, activating the brain in ways other discourses cannot.

YOU ARE THE PERSON RESPONSIBLE

A central premise in my work is that each of us can become the master of our own destiny. This became clearer to me in my early 40s while I was attending an intense 4-day self-improvement training. Each day we went until we were done, a decision the trainer made. It was often midnight, or beyond, before a session closed. On one of these days I was standing in the group of about 200 people having a conversation with the trainer. In a variety of ways he was trying to tell me that I was responsible for my life. This came at a time when I was still whining about my illegitimate birth and many years in orphanages. People around me got what the trainer was saying. I did not.

Later that day each of us was instructed to lie on the carpeted hotel room floor, totally relax, close our eyes, and entertain any images that surfaced. I saw myself as a sperm racing up the fallopian tubes, and being the winner, entered the waiting egg. I lay there in amazement, pondering the image and what it might mean. Finally I understood that it was not the act of insemination out of wedlock for which I was responsible but my experience of that chapter in my life.

I mention this because if there is any central message I would like to impart to others, it is that each of us is responsible for the way we deal with the circumstance of our lives. Academics describe this as perceived self-efficacy; a person's beliefs about their abilities to produce desired levels of performance that influence events that affect their lives. Self-efficacy beliefs determine how people feel, think, self-motivate, and behave. Efficacy is the single most powerful energy fund in high-performing teachers and students (Bandura, 1997). This idea of self-efficacy is captured in cancer survivor Portia Nelson's (2012) five-stanza piece titled "There's a Deep Hole in the Sidewalk." She begins:

Chapter One

I walk down the street

There is a deep hole in the sidewalk. I fall in.

I am lost . . . I am helpless

It isn't my fault

It takes forever to find a way out

The next three chapters capture her increasing sense of responsibility and reactions to what is occurring. Her final chapter reads:

Chapter Five

I walk down a different street.

While I was in my 70s my family invited me to write a memoir about my childhood. After much resistance I did. The result of writing *I Don't Do That Anymore* (Garmston, 2011) was to free me from the effects of my childhood.

In my early 80s I found myself in a hospital clinic for patients with emphysema. Trying to come to grips with the fact that my lifestyle had indeed led to this result, I wrote a poem titled *Wheezer* (Appendix). The poem starts "not his fault/he insisted," suggesting the struggle many of us have in being accountable for our fates.

This book is designed to be accessible according to your interest and style. You might choose to read sequentially or sample areas of greatest interest in no particular order. While no one section is dependent on knowing the earlier ones, the book as a whole will answer the what, the why, and the how of persuasive storytelling. Use the Table of Contents, Guide To Story Locations and Story Categories and/or summaries below to get a sense of where you might like to begin.

Four speakers of different genders, races, and styles are assembled within this book for you to watch. Two are professional storytellers (few of us will reach this level), and two are speakers who use stories embedded in their presentations. These presentations can be easily located in the table of contents with this icon ▭ and can be watched online using the links and QR codes provided.

☐ FREE GROUP FACILITATION STUDY GUIDE

For readers interested in extending their learning and skills development, a Storytelling Study Companion by Robert Garmston and Michael Dolcemascolo can be accessed online. More information is available in this section at the end of the book.

NAVIGATING THIS BOOK

Should you encounter stories you might like to come back to or use at some time, I suggest marking the page with a Post-it note. You can also search for story title or function using the Story Categories and Guide to Story Locations. Stories are organized into four functions or purposes: shifting perceptions, inviting learning, inspiring action, and seeking desired states.

SHIFT PERCEPTIONS	INVITE LEARNING	INSPIRE ACTION	SEEK A DESIRED STATE
These stories invite listeners to move beyond current frames of reference, to entertain new ways of observing and interpreting their worlds.	These tales offer learning opportunities about presentation skills, courage, and internal processes.	This set of stories inspires, encourages, and reveals how leaders influence those around them.	These stories illustrate ways presenters and leaders lead others to more productive states, attitudes, and behaviors than what currently exists.

THE BOOK IN THREE PARTS

Part I: Why Stories Work

Data do not move people. Stories do. Not just any story, but stories constructed to entertain, sway, encourage, and motivate have an uncanny effect on attitudes and even behaviors. Most people suffer from information overload through digital umbilical cords, their moment-to-moment lifeline to the world. Messages intended to influence us have a dismal rate of effectiveness with the exception of messages sent through the oldest communication pipelines in the world—gossip, rumors, and stories. Whether orally delivered, read, heard around a fire, or seen on a screen, psychologists, public speakers, and teachers laud the astonishing effectiveness of story. Students inhale tales that motivate and demonstrate values and ways of behaving, and similar learning occurs for adults.

Chapter 1 summarizes reasons for stories and the value of telling them. Chapter 2 reveals neurological findings about what happens in the brain when a well-constructed story changes perceptions, attitudes, and even behaviors. The story of how neurochemicals in the brain induce empathy and efforts to help others is told here.

Part II: Find, Design, and Deliver Your Story

Chapter 3 invites readers to find their own stories from their life and work experiences and reveals how the components of many types of stories—work culture, personal, historical, even hysterical—can be structured to persuade. Chapter 4 identifies where you might find six categories accessible to everyone. All cultures teach values and reinforce norms through story. This chapter illustrates some stories from various cultures and ways they guide their people. The last class of story presented in this chapter is metaphor, the importance and structures of which are detailed in Chapter 5.

Steps for preparing a story are described in Chapter 6, as well as seven desirable features to include: How you enter the story is important—how you begin—and suitable exits are equally as significant. Features of effective stories are described here, and, as the TV commercials say, "so much more." Part of the "more" is how your selection of words can cause listeners to actually experience what you are telling them, a necessary component to move people to action. Seven steps to preparing a story are described. Finally, Part II concludes at Chapter 7 with instructions about how to deliver a story.

Part III: Changing Behaviors With Story

Storytelling should exist in every organization, says Carpenter (2015). This section reveals why. Storytelling is now at the forefront in many business conversations. Microsoft, Verizon, Nike, and Boeing have all created the role of Chief Storyteller. United Airlines, one of the most recent companies to create this position, hired a new "crew member," Dana Brooks Reinglass, to fulfill that role. A recent Adidas job ad even listed "storyteller" among the traits the company was looking for in hiring Chicago-area store managers (Zumbach, 2016).

Chapter 8 addresses resistance and how it is best acknowledged. A simple mental model is introduced that shapes the trajectory of all stories designed to improve attitudes and behaviors. Three examples show how this model can be used, one an interaction with an angry parent, one a story spun to redirect the counterproductive energies of a group, and one a story told to an assistant superintendent that helped her improve her work performance.

Possibly the most important concept of all is presented in Chapter 9, meeting groups where they are in the moment without judgment, with full acceptance, but with a plan to carry them forward to better states. Chapter 10 deepens understandings developed in Chapter 2 about the neuroscience of listening to stories. Using research on brain functioning, this chapter offers six tools for story structures capable of transforming existing states into more desirable ones.

In Chapter 11, two stories illustrate change-producing tales. Advanced conditions for a well-formed story are presented. These include mechanisms to bypass defensive filters, strategies to embed indirect suggestions, and the critical role of verifiable data. A reference is made to the Appendix, where readers will see a detailed description of how these features were embedded in the first story. Chapter 12 summarizes key understandings.

Forty stories are presented in a Story Catalog. They are organized according to purpose: stories to shift perceptions, invite learning, inspire action, and lead to a desired state.

A Guide to Story Locations is offered so that readers can find specific stories to review.

APPENDIX

Worksheets are provided on several topics, including metaphor and desired-state stories.

ACKNOWLEDGMENTS

I have been blessed with a procession of gracious teachers at every stage of my life. From childhood, my social worker Marabel Beck and her husband Bob, who provided me with the first positive adult male relationship by allowing me to work on his dairy farm. Also in childhood King and Alice Hart, who became my foster parents when the children's home I was in would no longer put up with me. They formally adopted me when I was 60, which is a story in itself. I've been exposed to a legion of luminaries in education and psychology and countless leaders in education. One of these, Robin Cano, formerly assistant superintendent in the Marin County district where she mentored me, has come into my life again. In her mid-90s, she is still sharp, inquisitive, and learning. She was the first to model leadership attributes and has influenced my orientation to serving students and others through the processes of leading. Most important is my wife, Sue, who for nearly 40 years has supported me, put up with me, partnered with me, loved me, and taught me everything I know about family.

Finally, my daughter Wendy Ferguson has also been my teacher, beginning when she was just 10 years of age and blessed with uncommon perception and wisdom for one so young. I continue to learn from her, most particularly as she has read this manuscript several times, offering reactions. Her contributions are legion. Any errors are mine. To each of you my deepest thanks.

Robert J. Garmston
El Dorado Hills, California

PUBLISHER'S ACKNOWLEDGMENTS

Corwin gratefully acknowledges the contributions of the following reviewers

Carolee Hayes
Director of Thinking Collaborative
Highlands Ranch, CO

Madeleine Hewitt
Executive Director of Schools
Athens, Greece

Nicole Mungo
Teacher of Computer Science and Business Education
Charlotte, NC

Louis Lim
Vice Principal
Richmond Hill, ON, Canada

Keith Mason
Professor and Researcher of Linguistics
New Providence, NJ

ABOUT THE AUTHOR AND ILLUSTRATOR

Robert J. Garmston is Emeritus Professor of Educational Administration at California State University, Sacramento. He is co-developer of Cognitive Coaching with Art Costa and co-developer of Adaptive Schools with Bruce Wellman. He has worked as an educational consultant and made presentations and conducted workshops for teachers, administrators, and staff developers on leadership, learning, and personal and organizational development in 24 countries on five continents. Formerly an administrator and teacher in Saudi Arabia and the United States, his work has been translated into Arabic, Dutch, Hebrew, Italian, and Spanish.

Bob lives in El Dorado Hills, California, near his five children and five (bright and cute) grandchildren.

fabobg@gmail.com

https://en.wikipedia.org/wiki/Robert_Garmston

Dede Tisone was a public school art teacher who has drawn her way around the world and is now living in San Francisco, California. She is currently working on a series of drawings about the homeless in San Francisco. Her drawings have been recently published in the *San Francisco Chronicle* and The Street Sheets.

http://www.dedetisone.com/

PART I

WHY STORIES WORK

Chapter 1 summarizes reasons for stories and the value of telling them. Chapter 2 reveals neurological findings about what happens in the brain when a well-constructed story changes perceptions, attitudes, and even behaviors. The story of how neurochemicals in the brain induce empathy and efforts to help others is told here.

1

WHY TELL STORIES

Data are a poor instrument for influence. At the time I am writing this, the United States Supreme Court is hearing a case about political gerrymandering and complaining that the statistical analysis they are receiving is hard to understand. The chief justice called it sociological gobbledygook. A school board in Minnesota was unmoved by a statistical analysis of free and reduced lunch students in the district but took action based on the stories of just two of these students. Jennifer Aaker, a professor of marketing at the Stanford Graduate School of Business, says that people remember information when it is weaved into narratives "up to 22 times more than facts alone" (Delistraty, 2014).

This chapter explores why stories are such a potent form of persuasion for teachers, leaders, and presenters and what happens in the minds of listeners that make them so.

The importance of stories—and by extension, allegories and metaphors—is indisputable. These are the things we remember, that stick in our minds. Fables, myths, and parables are what all great teachers use—from Plato's allegory of the cave to stories in the Quran about the prophet Muhammad, to creation stories in the Hindu Vedas, to Jesus's parables to Tolkien's Ring stories and even J. K. Rowling's Harry Potter tales. Milton Erickson, considered the most influential hypnotherapist of his time, told stories. Stories were at times his primary mode of therapy. Over 100 of his stories, presented verbatim, can be found in *My Voice Will Go*

LET ME TELL YOU A STORY

Susan stood before a classroom of people who didn't want to be there. When she greeted them, only half the group made eye contact. Their boss had directed them to attend and most felt it was a waste of time. Desperate, and momentarily inspired, Susan said, "Let me tell you a story." At the word story, *heads jerked up and everyone was riveted. She proceeded to tell the story of the U.S. Navy ship* Vincennes *in the Persian Gulf that misidentified Iran Air Flight 655 as an aggressive military plane and shot it down. This was 1988; Iran and Iraq were at war. Tensions were high. Susan's story served her purpose of exploring the role of human error in disasters. During the remainder of the class the group was focused and engaged* (Fisher, 2013).

With You: Teaching Tales of Milton Erickson, edited with comments by Rosen (1982).

Why are stories so influential? They teach, persuade, and enforce group beliefs and norms. They are uniquely effective because (1) they stimulate neurological changes that increase empathy; (2) they personalize presentation content, sending forth a gossamer filament that connects the audience and the presenter; (3) they open windows to the intuitive knowledge of an audience; and (4) they can tap the resources of the unconscious mind.

Facts, data, theories, and statistics contribute richly to learning but can be read in any book, heard on any audiotape, and seen on any screen. Stories, however, transcend learning from facts to knowing in a personal way. In part this occurs in response to the presenter's nonverbal behaviors. Voice pattern, tone, inflection, facial expression, gestures, and use of floor space shift the listener's experience. When you tell a story, the audience sees, hears, and feels more of the narrative.

Stories also tap the wells of intuitive knowledge humans possess. We know in at least three ways: (1) rationally, aided by our logical and often linear thinking processes; (2) empirically, by what we feel and see and hear; and (3) metaphorically—to know something metaphorically is to understand it intuitively. Stories open us up to the symbolic dimensions of experience and to the multiple meanings that may coexist, each giving extra shades of meaning to the other.

Finally, a certain type of story can engage our unconscious minds in ways that bring resolution to problems, shift us from distressed emotional states to more positive ones, offer resources for self-healing, and change the way a group behaves. Such stories have existed for thousands of years in many cultures. It is only recently that psychologists and linguists have identified what it is about certain stories that so productively engage the unconscious. Some stories speak first to the right hemisphere of the brain, activating images and emotions that are then communicated in word symbols to the slightly more ponderous left hemisphere of the brain, which hears them as if it had heard them before. In Chapter 8, I describe the linguistic and physiological mechanisms for this. Here, I mention two remarkable books that describe the process: David Gordon's *Therapeutic Metaphors* (1978/2017) and Joyce Mills and Richard Crowley's *Therapeutic Metaphors for Children and the Child Within* (1986/2014).

COMMUNICATION SUFFOCATION

Stories influence each of us in ways most other forms of communication cannot. We are bombarded with inputs in which the messages rarely get through. This is one reason that stories matter, because they slip through the normal filters muting other messages. Recently my wife and I were searching the web for information about a place to holiday. We encountered information about geography, culture, history, agriculture, natural resources, monetary systems, customs, weather, and national products, as well as hotel and transport options. All we wanted to know was where we might see wildlife near our destination. This experience reminded me of the wealth of information available to one who searches. More challenging is the information we do not search for, yet get anyway in the form of ads, pop-ups, phone solicitations, news outlets, and even unrequested information from places of work or worship. Much of what is transmitted we receive blurrily or at low volume because we are not interested.

LEADING THROUGH NARRATIVE

When Mark Graham was commanding general at Fort Carson, Colorado, he told a story to his senior staff, even cried while telling it, and launched a transformation of how the base—and ultimately how the Army—treated suicides.

Fort Carson had an unusually high suicide rate. Graham had recently lost two sons, both in the Army, one to suicide and the other to combat in Iraq. He talked openly about PTSD and wept in front of soldiers while speaking. Some thought the tears were an indication of weakness. Only later did the soldiers realize that his willingness to cry was a strength.

Graham set up a phone line to which people could call any hour of the day or night. A trusted sergeant would decide which calls to forward. In one case a mother called saying she couldn't reach her son. He was depressed, and she was worried. The call was relayed to Graham, who had the soldier removed from the barracks and saw that he entered therapy. The soldier survived.

Of enormous value, Graham created the concept of an Embedded Behavioral Health Team in which a clinical professional would be assigned to a brigade at all times. When the brigade deploys to a war zone, the doctor goes with them. Graham, now retired, serves as the senior director of the Rutgers University Behavioral Health Care National Call Center and the Director of VETS4WARRIORS (Dreazen, 2015).

Major General Graham's practice in leading through narrative is just one example of how leaders—in all fields and at all levels within organizations—can stimulate positive change.

> *Story is the only way to activate parts of the brain so that listeners turn the story into their own idea and experience.*
>
> Uri Hasson of Princeton

As we transition from a market economy to a network economy, the volume and pace of communication increase. Because of the complexities in the modern world, everyone is influenced and, at times, seeks to influence the beliefs, values, goals, and tools of others.

Television stories sell. Producers have become increasingly sophisticated in using narrative to market goods and services. Some observe that this is because of the way brains operate—we think in stories. While many ads display for only 15 seconds, others run 90 seconds, giving time for the marketer's theme to develop. Drug company ads are especially noticeable because their voiceovers detail the various negative side effects a drug may carry while a story plays out on the screen to distract us. The story usually features several smiling people happy and fully enjoying life. The real message is "Don't worry. Be happy! Oh, and use this medication."

Storytelling skills for leaders have become a regular feature in periodicals and seminars because stories sell ideas as well as products. You may have experienced an insurance salesperson tell you a story about unexpected catastrophes related to the product for sale. The message is "Be proactively wise and protect yourself from the unpredictable . . . by investing in this product." My grandson Ethan, on a break from college, showed up the other day to sell me a household product. Telling stories was part of the pitch he'd been taught. I was surprised when a few days later my second grandson Sean approached me with the same product and pitch.

As another example of story power, a number of history teachers are harnessing the musical *Hamilton* to inspire their students. Through the rap, students learn that the figures in the Revolutionary War were real people with real feelings, strengths, and weaknesses. The Gilder Lehrman Institute of American History has actually created a study guide for students based on this musical (R. Patterson, 2017).

 WATCH A STORY BEING TOLD

 https://youtu.be/Zkb-zg4JCLk

When beginning this book, it may be useful to see a 4-minute example of exemplary storytelling by Meghan Markle. When she made this 2015 speech on gender equity, Markle was best known for playing the role of paralegal Rachel Zane on *Suits*. At the time of this writing, she's just married Prince Harry. Markle has her own style and, unlike most of us, was trained as an actor. So the purpose of viewing this piece is not to emulate what she does but to notice generalizable storytelling qualities. Each of us has our own individualized mannerisms, voice, and personality, and that is who our audiences want to hear.

The speech is exceptional in its construction. Her opening line tells you this is going to be a story, the narrative includes tension and surprise, and she closes with a simple call to action. Her presence, like the best speakers, seems more a conversation with the audience than a presentation. She is congruently expressive in voice, face, eyes, hands, and posture. She speaks in an unhurried pace, noticeably pausing between thoughts. Readers are invited to return to this video when examining the parts of this book that deal with story construction and delivery.

Chapter 6 describes story construction, and Chapter 7 addresses delivery.

HOW STORYTELLING BEGAN

Listening to stories has been a sacred rite of communication since the sun first rose over human existence. The earliest people told stories to share and interpret experience. An early benefit might have been learning from failure. An unsuccessful hunting story told at the end of the day might have carried cues from which insights could be gained about more effective hunting practices. Stories within indigenous groups are known for common themes such as coming of age, morality, customs, and history.

Anthropologist Polly Wiessner (2014) lived in what is now Namibia among the Ju/'hoansi people, when they still existed by hunting and gathering. She coded conversations involving at least five people. Day talk, she discovered, was quite different from talk at night around a fire. She identified 34% of daytime talk as criticism, complaint, or conflict, including workplace political debates. But when the sun went down and the people gathered to reflect on their experiences, the talk was transformed. Most of the time people told stories about people they knew, information about earlier generations, and what might be happening in other villages or the spirit world. This kind of talk took 81% of the Ju/'hoansi's communal time.

Figure 1.1   Differences in Day- and Nighttime Talk Among the Ju/'hoansi

Daytime Talk	Nighttime Talk
34% Criticism, complaint, conflict	81% Information and inspiration

The purposes of stories for indigenous peoples were often to instruct children about cultural values and proper ways to live. The meanings of these stories were not always explicit, and children were expected to make their own meaning, deriving general principles for their lives. A brilliant modern equivalent of this practice is presented in the film *A Monster Calls* (Ness, 2016). It tells the story of a child whose mother is terminally ill. One night, the child (Conor MacDougal) is visited by a giant tree-like monster who states that he will come back and tell him three stories. I was stunned, as were psychologist friends of mine, by the beauty and power of this film, which leads Conor to tell a terrible truth, a revelation necessary to set him free.

Today 370 million indigenous people continue to maintain their cultural identity around the world through stories. It's estimated that in 70 countries, from the Arctic to the South Pacific, these groups retain distinct characteristics different from those of the national majority. Examples include populations in the Americas (the Lakota in the United States, the Mayas in Guatemala, and the Aymaras in Bolivia), in the circumpolar region (the Inuit and Aleutians), in northern Europe (the Saami), in Australia (the Aborigines or peoples indigenous to mainland Australia or the island of Tasmania and Torres Strait Islanders), and in New Zealand (the Maori).

The stories came in all varieties: myths, legends of all kinds, fairy tales, trickster stories, fables, ghost tales, hero stories, and epic adventures. Stories were told, retold, and passed down through generations, reflecting the cumulative wisdom and knowledge of early people.

There are tales used to explain important but often confusing events and natural disasters in those early times, for example, fires, storms, thunder, floods, tidal waves, lightning, and so on. It was common for people to believe in the stories of gods, which bound them to a common heritage and belief system. In fact, it is believed by most historians and psychologists that storytelling is one of the many things that define and bind our humanity. Humans are perhaps the only animals that create and tell stories.

So it appears that stories have been essential to human existence since its infancy. In all cultures, in all ages, storytelling has been the vehicle for human reflection on experience, an ability that separates us from other life forms. Stories also help us remember data better than a presentation of facts and are more persuasive to listeners than advice. Through stories, listeners adopt ideas as if they were their own.

But the picture of why stories matter is not yet complete. Crucial to understanding the role of stories in our lives is understanding something about what stories do to our brains. That's the topic of the next chapter.

2

THE
NEUROSCIENCE
OF NARRATIVE

"Once upon a time . . ." a woman told a story to a large audience.

Within a month she received—are you ready?—a million dollars!

Inside the room, 30 faces fix intently on the speaker. The words "once upon a time" evoke a light trance. The audience sits, bodies expectant, breathing slowly as pond water, their faces like photographs of themselves as young children. They are waiting, imagining the next development of the speaker's story, open to new discovery, imaginations liberated.

Stories hold our attention better than other forms of transmitting information. Attention is in short supply because it is costly to a brain needing to conserve resources. Tension draws in the mind, and if a story does not maintain our attention, the brain will look for something else to do: Did I feed the dog this morning? The hair on that man looks like a wig. Better check my smartphone. Wonder if I can meet Gilbert at lunch? Even in well-told stories the brain will occasionally drift, do a quick search of the environment, then return to the story as the tension rises.

Effective stories also produce something psycholinguists call *transportation*, when one loses oneself in the flow of the narrative. Watch the absorption of an audience as professional storyteller Diane Ferlatte (2013) tells stories at the International Storytelling Conference *Many Stories but One World*.

A STORY WORTH WATCHING

https://youtu.be/iduMoffZ_54

Ferlatte is at the peak of accomplishment as a professional storyteller, and her inclusion here should be taken as a model to which one might aspire.

Paying attention is not easy. Without tension it is not possible.

STORIES AROUSE
COOPERATIVE INSTINCTS

Measuring the moment-to-moment degree of attention listeners have when hearing stories, Paul Zak (2014), director of the Center for Neuroeconomics Studies at Claremont Graduate School, found that a good story causes changes in brain activity. In what he describes as an "amazing neural ballet," hearing a story produces a neurochemical called oxytocin in the blood stream. Oxytocin is produced when we are trusted or shown a kindness. It motivates cooperation with others. It enhances our ability to experience others' emotions. The amount of oxytocin in the blood is predictive of how much people are motivated to help others. Because nursing mothers secrete this neurochemical, it is sometimes called the *bonding chemical* or *empathy chemical.*

Zak (2014) suggests this so-called empathy chemical might be the neurological basis for the golden rule, because it promotes behaviors intended to help others. Another of his findings is that certain portions of the brain experience heightened connectivity, even by reading a story. Reading simple, humanistic stories changes what is in our blood streams. In one study, blood samples were taken before and after reading a story about a father and his terminally ill son. Levels of oxytocin (empathy) and cortisol (which reduces the negative responses to stress) both increased after reading the story. Subjects were then asked to donate money to a cause for ill children. The higher amount of cortisol was correlated to larger contributions (Lieberman, 2013).

Many experiments in which oxytocin was safely introduced into hundreds of people's brains have demonstrated the positive affect on prosocial behaviors like giving donations. In one experiment Zak (2014) and his team introduced a placebo into the brains of a control group and synthetic oxytocin into the brains of an experimental group. Both groups were exposed to 16 public service announcements of 30 to 60 seconds on topics like smoking, drinking to excess, speeding, and global warming. Later, after being asked for donations, the group that received oxytocin donated, on average, 56% more money to charity compared with participants who received the placebo. But why? The oxytocin group showed substantially more concern for the characters in the stories than did the placebo group. This concern motived them to donate money to charities that could alleviate the suffering those stories depicted even though they knew the characters were professional actors.

Figure 2.1   Oxytocin and the Brain

The Production of Oxytocin

- Oxytocin and attention are increased when a story includes tension.
- When attention is maintained, it's more likely that listeners will share the emotions of the main characters. When people share the emotions, it's more likely they will mimic the character's feelings and behaviors.
- Listening to a character story like this causes oxytocin to be released.
- When oxytocin is released, it's more likely that people will trust the storyteller and take whatever action the storyteller suggests.

$ $ $ THE MILLION-DOLLAR STORY

A musician in Melbourne posted a video on Kickstarter in 2012. It showed her holding up a number of handmade signs explaining that she had spent 4 years developing some songs and had left her record label. Now she was asking for help to continue her work. Within 30 days she received $1.2 million. Over 24,000 viewers preordered the album. Some contributed artwork. Some sent gifts. This woman, Amanda Palmer, was successful, not by asking for funds, but by telling a story. You can see her on a TED Talk describing the whole affair (Palmer, 2013).

Stories have two other advantages over data when the intent is to understand and/or persuade. First, they can be compelling because they mimic the way our brains work. Stories have been described as simply cause and effect. We think in narratives. I notice myself thinking, for example, that when the weather cools today, I will take the dog for a walk. After that I will fix dinner.

Throughout our waking hours, much of the chatter in our brains takes the form of stories.

The second advantage held by stories is that they encourage our brains to simulate what we are hearing, mimicking the feelings, pictures, and sounds described in the story. We can't listen to a story about a waterfall without activating the very parts of the brain that would be engaged if, in actuality, we were there. Brain scans show that when we visualize a locomotive, the visual cortex lights up. When we imagine someone's arm on our shoulder, tactile areas of the brain are activated. People who imagine they are looking at the Eiffel Tower can't resist their eyes moving up (Heath & Heath, 2007). As consumers of stories, we seem to become participants, not observers.

> *Readers unconsciously invent parts that are missing in stories.*

The Heath brothers (2007, p. 209) report a remarkable phenomenon that illustrates the process of simulation. Participants in a study were divided into two groups. One group read a story in which a critical object was *associated* with the central character in the story. "John *put on* his sweatshirt before he went jogging." The second group read a story in which the same critical object was *separated* from the main character. "John *took off* his sweatshirt before he went jogging." Two sentences later the story made another reference to the sweatshirt and the computer measured how much time it took people to read that sentence. The people who thought John took off the sweatshirt took longer to read that sentence than the people who thought he had it on.

The readers who thought John took off the sweatshirt needed more time than the other group because they had to play out a scenario in their mind of what John did (where he left the sweat-shirt) whereas the other group did not (he had the sweatshirt on all the time). The authors offer this as an example of the simulations we do in our minds in relation to story.

Figure 2.2   Simulations Readers Perform When Reading

Takes Less Time to Read	Takes Longer to Read
Because the readers knew he had the sweatshirt on all the time they didn't have to make images in their minds of what he did with it.	Because readers had to play out a scenario in their minds of what John did, where he left the sweatshirt, etc.
"John *put on* his sweatshirt before he went jogging."	"John *took off* his sweatshirt before he went jogging."
A critical object was *associated* with the central character in the story.	The same critical object was *separated* from the main character.

DESIRED-STATE STORIES

Similar brain activity occurs when ambiguous or confusing terms are used because the listeners must go inside to search for mean-ings. This becomes a factor in stories designed to speak to the subliminal mind and is explored in Chapter 8. Certain stories can influence perceptions or change behavior. I told a story once to a friend and borrowed her metaphor of being lost in a darkly dense forest. I extended her metaphor to include a leaden gray cloud cover. The traveler in this story knew that above that dreary layer shone a bright and brilliant sky. Sometime later, she told me this part of the story lifted her mood, shifted her perspective, and revealed options she hadn't previously seen.

WETTING THE BED NO MORE

In *Therapeutic Metaphors for Children and The Child Within* (Mills & Crowley, 2014) the authors give examples of ways therapeutic stories have helped children change behaviors. A favorite of mine is a boy who continued to wet his bed long beyond the age when that was normal. *He was told a story about a baby circus elephant who was learning to hold water in his trunk. One day—you know where this is going—a fire broke out on the other side of the circus. Little elephant got his trunk full of water and— this is the important part—had to hold it because it was a long way to get to the fire. He was successful. The fire was extinguished and the boy no longer wet his bed.*

These stories, which I call *desired-state stories*, invoke another mental process. In what is known as *transderivational searches* (see a definition in Chapter 10), listeners search their own experiences for events that might mirror what they hear in the story.

Attention, it turns out, is not under our conscious control. Stories, however, capture our full focus. They initiate a chemical dance within the brain responsible for such prosocial human attributes as empathy, kindness, and cooperation. Referred to as the father of neuroscience, Ramon y Cajal (1852–1934) observed through the brain's chemical and electrical processes neurons touch without touching, communicating across infinitesimal gaps. Later we learned that listeners' brains actually become synchronized with the brain of the storyteller and internal experiences of the story are created in images, feelings, and sounds so profoundly it is as if the story has come alive inside us. Story is a mechanism by which listeners adopt ideas as their own (Swanson, Newman, Araque, & Dubinsky, 2017).

Chapter 8 gives several examples of desired-state experiences for adults and reveals how to design them. On several occasions I have been able to change the behaviors of a group with this type of story. Reading on, you will find that you also will be able to influence behaviors of a group you are with by using a well-designed story.

iStock.com/A-R-T-U-R

iStock.com/Julichka

PART II

FIND, DESIGN, AND DELIVER YOUR STORY

You already tell stories to friends, partners, children, co-workers, and new acquaintances, whether you think of yourself as a storyteller or not. To extend your current capacities, the next two chapters will help you search your own work life, family, and recreations for story content. You will identify sources to borrow from within six distinct categories and adapt tales for your purposes. You will discover certain features essential to effective stories and learn about a special story type—a signature story—that is exclusively about you.

3

FINDING PERSONAL STORIES

NO TRUCK WITH ADMINISTRATORS

It was August, muggy and hot. I had just arrived in Saudi Arabia to begin a job as principal, and I was making the rounds, introducing myself to teachers as they worked in their classrooms preparing for the opening of school. I remember one teacher in particular. I greeted her as I had others, offering my name and announcing that I would be the new principal at the school. Barely looking at me she said, "Well, I've never had no truck with administrators." Thus began my knowledge of the work culture at this school and suggested the tensions ahead.

This chapter offers suggestions for locating story ideas within your personal experiences, both at work and in life. The next chapter extends the search to other sources. Both chapters are organized around four story intentions. The four intentions are displayed in Table 3.1.

STORY CATEGORIES

Table 3.1   Sources of Personal Stories

SHIFT PERCEPTIONS	INVITE LEARNING	INSPIRE ACTION	SEEK A DESIRED STATE
These stories invite listeners to move beyond current frames of reference and to entertain new ways of observing and interpreting their worlds.	These tales offer learning opportunities about presentation skills, courage, and internal processes.	This set of stories inspires, encourages, and reveals how leaders influence those about them.	These stories illustrate ways to lead others to more productive states, attitudes, and behaviors than what currently exists.

All four categories below can be used in any of the four classes above.

Life Experiences

Work Experiences

Signature Stories

Organization or Work Culture Stories

Often the most persuasive yarns come from personal experiences or an anecdote someone has told us in informal conversation. The story at the beginning of this chapter is an example that I might extend to make a point about the work culture in this school. When your radar is keen for story content, you'll collect these for later development.

The sources for personal stories are all aspects of your life. Your early childhood, adolescent years, and experiences as a student can be particularly poignant, because they help audiences connect with the child in us all. Your family, recreational pursuits, and times of adversity are great corners into which to peek for story content. When telling a story of personal adversity, make it useful by telling the group what you learned from it. Often we learn more from failures than from successes.

Stories are told for enjoyment, entertainment, to make a point, or to invite curiosity. I've watched a number of presenters and administrators tell stories with specific intention: sometimes to invite new perceptions, promote learning, inspire others to action, or even change behaviors.

LOCATING PERSONAL STORY MATERIAL

Any one of the four major categories in Table 3.1 could also be a *signature story*. This is a story about something that is autobiographically you, that contributes to your uniqueness, and that illustrates a theme in your life. Signature stories can be told many times, to many different audiences, and could live within your tales of life experience, work experience, or organization and/or work culture.

If you've ever heard the poet Maya Angelou speak, then you probably heard her tell about her childhood and being raised by a relative of hers in the South. If you are like me, you've probably not thought of your life as having a signature story. Odds are good that you do have one. A story of stealing my birth certificate to learn the names of my biological parents (which I did at age 16) could be an example of a signature story.

Signature stories need to be handled carefully. Their purpose is not to adorn oneself with mystique or sympathy but to illustrate a specific point. To accomplish this requires a certain level of detachment, as if you are reporting events, not reliving them. I think, too, that the signature story is probably more appropriate for keynote speeches than for presentations to smaller groups. Here's why. While General Mark Graham's experience talking about his son's suicide is an exception to this, leaders in small groups may often maintain some distance from those reporting to them, keeping lines of authority clear. In contrast, speakers at large events usually work to decrease the psychological distance between themselves and an audience. Signature stories do this well.

Desired-state stories acknowledge without judgment a current counterproductive mood or emotion, set conditions for self-directed change, then offer a pathway to more resourceful states. This story type uses a process called *pace and lead* (Costa & Garmston, 2016). These are formative narratives, stories that encourage listeners to move beyond their current states into more productive ones. One way to think about pacing is linking what you say to the experiences of the audience as if metaphorically walking alongside them. This is a way of acknowledging the validity of the listener's subjective experience. Without starting where a person is in the moment, it's awfully hard to lead him or her to more productive states.

Dolan (2017) offers a way to locate experiences—at work or beyond—from which you might spin a profitable yarn. In one approach, you list your jobs looking for experiences in one of the four categories you wish to use. No job is too long ago or too small. Vignettes like this next one can be told to any group by simply changing the "my" to "a person I know."

One of my early jobs was picking prunes. The children's home in which I lived sent groups of us out to nearby orchards. For weeks we labored in the hot sun. We earned a quarter a box, and on a dusty, dry, backbreaking day the oldest and best of us could earn up to $8. My guess is that even on our worst day, we can continue pushing as the kids did in the prune orchard. This type of story might be used in a team meeting to inspire action.

Dolan (2017) developed a search model for experiences that might yield useful leadership stories. In her work she suggests that for each job you list, you identify several experiences that might serve as genesis for a story and classify these by theme. To illustrate this idea, experiences from several of my circumstances appear in Table 3.2.

Table 3.2   Examples of Personal Stories

Purpose	Circumstance	Event
Shifting Perception	University Class	Graduate students are told a story about a bear pacing within its cage during and right after transit. When the cage was removed, the bear continued to pace within the exact limitations of its now nonexistent cage.

(Continued)

Table 3.2 (Continued)

Purpose	Circumstance	Event
Inviting Learning	Director of Instruction, Bellevue School District	I lobbied to hire a teacher. The interview team agreed with my assessment that she would be a good addition to the staff.
		Two weeks in, parents complained that she was spanking her second-grade students with a two-by-four. She was dismissed. We had failed to check her references.
Inspiring Action	Fifth-Grade Teacher, Marin County, CA	Dale played alone on the playground, often wearing an army helmet and carrying toy planes and cars. He was the butt of jokes from other kids. I taught a unit on scapegoating and then introduced a special form of baseball in which the goal was improvement, not winning. Encouragements were shouted at Dale when he was at bat or in the field. Class members increasingly accepted Dale.
Seeking a Desired State	Seminar Leader, Illinois summer session	I taught Days 8, 9, and 10 in a 10-day summer in-service program for high school teachers. They were disrespectful and inattentive to the previous instructors. I started with a story that resulted in dramatically significant improvements in their behavior.

STORIES ABOUT YOUR ORGANIZATION

A certain type of story lives in the work of organizations. These stories have two purposes: One is to symbolize the overarching goals and the values of the group; the other is to provide suggestions, through story, about how participants should act. Four characteristics set these stories apart from other types of culturally held stories.

1. *They are real.* They are told about real people, describe specific actions, convey a specific time and place, and are connected with the values of the organization.
2. *They are known.* People in the organization not only know the story, but they also know that others know it and act in accordance with its guidance.
3. *They are believed.* The point the story makes is believed to be true of the organization.
4. *It models the organization's norms.* The story describes how things are to be done and not done and describes associated rewards and punishments.

Organizational stories are often about the work culture, values, or related tensions normal to organizations: equality versus inequality, security versus insecurity, or independence versus interdependence. Popular management books like *Management by Storying Around: A New Method of Leadership* by David Armstrong (1992) and *A Passion for Excellence* by Nancy Austin and Tom Peters (1985) are usually filled with these types of stories. Here is an example from *A Passion for Excellence.*

DOMINO'S PIZZA

Domino's Pizza vice president Don Vlcek recalled the speed and impact with which a certain story traveled through his system. While visiting a distribution center he noticed some unacceptably lumpy dough. As he tells it, "The quality wasn't right. We couldn't let it go out. I stopped, I rolled up my sleeves, and I worked with the local team to fix the procedure. In twenty-four hours, the news had traveled twenty-five hundred miles! I got a call from one of my centers on the other side of the continent: 'Don, we heard about what you did. That's great. That's the kind of commitment to quality we need. We're behind you over here. We'll redouble our efforts.' You had to have been here to believe it." (Austin & Peters, 1985, pp. 329–330)

Peters and Austin added that they did believe it. Examples of stories like this running through an entire organization are not unusual.

Here's another organizational story from an elementary school in New York State. This was a school invested in interdependence. The story is told to parents and new hires. A third-grade student wrote to her principal. Some names have been changed but the spelling and capitalizations are as produced by the student.

IS THERE SOMETHING I CAN DO?

"I understand why I got in trouble but 3 WEEK'S DETENTION and NO RECESS is NOT FAIR. I know why I got in trouble. The reason why I got in trouble is because I was arguing with Monica and I was laughing at the funny dances Ms. Hunt was making. The 3-week's thing is unfair. 3 week's detention and 3 week's no recess is unfair. I've written a letter about the 3-week's thing and about what I understand. I'm just a kid I make mistakes too.

Is there something else I can do for the school instead of 3 weeks detention and 3 weeks no recess? Here are some things I would rather do than 3 weeks detention and 3 weeks no recess. I'll go to kindergarten and help with things. Like to help them be a better writer and to help them with their math. What if I help Mr. Clark serving lunch and putting garbage bags in the garbage. Ms. Adams has a lot of work to do, so I could help her. I can put stuff in the mailbox and I can pick up the phone and say, "name of school how may I help you"? I will tell Ms. Adams what the person needs then I will give her the phone. I WANT TO GIVE BACK TO THE SCHOOL!!"

Another example of a work culture story is this one, often referred to in meetings with new teachers, faculty meetings, and parent advisory group meetings.

CUTTING AIDE TIME

At one elementary school funds were cut for Title I instructional aides and the principal sought teacher input about how to implement this change. Teachers reported that they "felt like turkeys being asked to vote on the merits of Thanksgiving." No one really wanted his or her aide's time cut. One first-grade teacher was adamant: She would lose aide time "over my dead body." Six months later, this same teacher volunteered to share her classroom aide with a third-grade tutoring program "if it will really make a difference in those students' learning to read." (Garmston & Wellman, 1999)

What happened? Teachers were committed to common goals for students and collaborative discourse for themselves. They had learned to practice two different ways of talking—*dialogue (to understand)* and *discussion (to decide)*—and individually, they focused on their capacities for professional discourse and openly reflected on these to improve personal and collective practice.

FINDING YOUR PERSONAL STORIES

"Write them down" is the first tip I've learned from experienced speakers and storytellers when I've asked how to find stories. Dolan (2017, p. 28) offers a template for locating story content from personal experiences outside work. Table 3.2 shows how this could be used with the special categories I've added to her work.

Table 3.3   Categorizing Personal Experiences

Shifting Perception	What Was It Like for You?
	Long after my mother was gone, I did an exercise to remove some of my anger toward her. I asked, "What was it like for you when I was a child?" The immediate response I heard in my head was, "I never did want to have children." In that moment I was released of any bitterness, realizing that her behavior was not about me, and I felt sorrow for her.
Inviting Learning	Disliked by the Chair
	I was new to the department and discovered the chair seemed to have an issue with me, treating me disrespectfully. I had no idea what was going on but had just learned about paying attention to the classes of sensory words people used— auditory, kinesthetic, and visual. What I discovered is that Tom used almost exclusively auditory language. It made sense when I thought about it. His office was often dark, with music playing. I decided to use auditory language when around Tom. Soon, I was amazed to find he was starting to sound out my ideas and listen to my advice.
Inspiring Action	One Urge at a Time
	Quitting smoking was hard, but someone told me I just had to deal with it one urge at a time. I discovered that if I did not give in, the desire would pass. It took a full year for all the craving to leave.
Seeking a Desired State	The Neat Freak
	A woman who described herself as a "neat freak" consulted a therapist. He said, "Imagine you are sitting in your favorite chair. All around you the carpet is perfectly smooth with not a footprint anywhere. All the surfaces are clean without a speck of dust, and it means that everyone who loves you is no longer here." She lost her compulsion to clean.

Of personal stories there should be plenty. A TV police drama in the late '50s and early '60s closed each episode delivering this line: "There are eight million stories in the naked city. This has been one of them."

Nigerian author Chimamanda Ngozi Adichie (2009) tells about the danger of a single story causing listeners to improperly generalize (Africans are poor, Mexicans are lazy, Americans are rich) rather than be introduced to the rich complexity that is each of us.

This chapter introduces four categories of story with which leaders and presenters persuade: those that invite changes in perception or learning, and those that stimulate action and change. Three special types of tales are described: one that is all about you—a signature story; stories that stimulate changes from less effective to more effective perceptions or behaviors; and finally stories about work culture intended to introduce or reinforce norms and values.

Readers might use Tables 3.2 and 3.3 to locate some of their own personal stories in those categories and consider what might represent a unique signature story. Even student experiences can be turned into organizational stories, maintaining values for newcomers or existing teams, schools, or districts. Finally, beware the single story used to describe any person or group. This came home to me with a wallop reading the novel *Exile*, in which a character visits Palestine to learn information important to the plot (N. Patterson, 2007).

Of course, there are many sources of stories beyond your own biography. Chapter 4 identifies six places to look for stories or story fragments to borrow.

4

OTHER STORY SOURCES

S ome stories you hear are too good not to record and retell. I heard this story about perseverance from a teacher in an international school in Beijing. Craig (the teacher) was on a bus with his brother somewhere in China. It's typical, he says, for foreigners to be charged 10 times what locals are charged, and even residents from a nearby village may be treated as foreigners.

RIDING THE BUS

Ticket takers approached the rear of bus where the two brothers were sitting. Craig tells his brother, who is studying Spanish, to let him do all the talking.

The fare is demanded. Craig pounds the wall of the bus with his open hand, yells at the ticket takers that he is tired of being taken for a foreigner. He carries on for a few minutes in that mode.

The ticket takers are unimpressed, claim he is a foreigner, and demand the fare. Craig explodes again, bangs his hand on the wall, and with an angry voice and perfect Mandarin proclaims his legitimacy. He is sorry his appearance is so non-Chinese. Not his fault. Comes from a small village near Russia and has taken on some of those racial characteristics. Tells them about his village. Finally, ticket takers relent. But then they ask, what about this fellow here, traveling with you. Craig explains it is his cousin from the same village but he has not learned Mandarin and speaks only in the village dialect. The brother speaks Spanish and the ticket takers are satisfied, but perhaps still a bit skeptical. As the bus pulls away, a passenger taps Craig's shoulder. I come from that village you described. You have some of your facts wrong.

While the previous chapter offered ideas for mining your own experiences for story, you should feel free to borrow from other sources. Figure 4.1 lists six sources, and of course there are more. You can borrow stories directly or adapt them to your setting and purposes. Obviously it is important to cite sources.

SIX STORY SOURCES

Figure 4.1   Some Story Sources

Biographies

Films

Histories

Literature

Culturally Specific Tales

Figurative Language/Metaphor

BIOGRAPHIES

For teachers, landscapes of illuminating biographies exist. One example is *The Passage of Power* by Robert Caro (1990), which details the earliest years of the Johnson presidency when the civil rights legislation was passed. We learn about Johnson's insecurities as well as his prodigious energy and skill to persuade. Janet Mock's *Redefining Realness: My Path to Womanhood, Identity, Love & So Much More* (2014) reveals her story of growing up multiracial, poor, and transgender in America. It is a courageous and inspirational story promoting us all toward greater acceptance of each other—and ourselves. An excellent international example is Marjane Satrapi's acclaimed graphic memoir *Persepolis* (2004). It is the story of Satrapi's childhood and coming of age within a large and loving family in Tehran during the Islamic Revolution. She reveals the contradictions between public and private life in a country plagued by political upheaval and describes the self-imposed exile from her beloved homeland. It is the chronicle of a girlhood and adolescence at once outrageous and familiar, a young life entwined with the history of her country yet filled with the universal trials and joys of growing up.

FILMS AND TELEVISION

The possibilities for stories from this category are endless. Consider telling stories from motion pictures or what appears on television.

- *Sully*, the story of the American pilot Chesley Sullenberger, who became a hero after safely landing his damaged plane on the Hudson River, offers an example of principled perseverance against supervisors who wished to assign blame.
- *Manchester by the Sea* manifests the reality of situations in which no good options are available. Inspirational stories about equity and racial justice can be found in films like *Loving* and *Fences*.
- *Loving* is the true story of a couple whose arrest for interracial marriage in 1958 Virginia began a legal battle that would end in the Supreme Court in 1967.
- *Fences* is the August Wilson story of a working-class African American father trying to raise his family in the 1950s, while coming to terms with the events of his life.
- For examples of uncommon courage, see *The Zookeeper's Wife*.
- *Hidden Figures* documents the prejudice existing in NASA during the 1950s and how it risked underutilizing

the prodigious intelligence and talents of several African American women.

■ Even the old *I Love Lucy* show has value with zany vignettes that illustrate styles of managing conflict.

■ *Seinfeld* reruns use many wonderfully comic illustrations with which one could teach paraphrasing.

HISTORIES

Team of Rivals, by Doris Kearns Goodwin (2006), gives intimate details regarding each of the men who served on Lincoln's first cabinet and offers understandings about the tensions and issues during the time of our Civil War.

Danger Close, by Amber Smith (2016), is an account of her experiences as one of the few women to fly the Kiowa Warrior helicopter in combat. Smith deployed to Iraq and Afghanistan and rose to Pilot-in-Command and Air Mission Commander in the premier Kiowa unit in the Army. She learned how to perform and survive under extreme pressure, both in action against an implacable enemy and within the elite "boy's club" of Army aviation.

Further away, historical novels like *Genghis: Birth of an Empire* by Conn Iggulden (2007) are irreplaceable for insights into the times and life of the steppes and beyond, giving vivid examples of ingenuity, adaptivity, creativity, courage, and warfare. Another rich find is *Shantaram* (2005), set in modern India, by Gregory David Roberts. This book is a history of sorts that might be thought of as an autobiographical novel. These stories are so rich you can experience the smells of Bombay, feel the pride and resilience of people living in the most extreme poverty, and learn about customs, criminals, and culture in India.

LITERATURE

Take your pick. Life is a library. Jane Austen, William Shakespeare, Laura Esquivel, Charles Dickens, Maya Angelou, Miguel de Cervantes, Mark Twain, Mario Vargas Llosa, J. K. Rowling, Ernest Hemingway, George Orwell, Franz Kafka, Paulo Coelho, Emily Dickinson, John Steinbeck, Leo Tolstoy, Toni Morrison, Jorge Luis Borges, and Donald Duck.

STORIES UNIQUE TO A PARTICULAR CULTURE

The tales in this group may be allegorical, may record a historical event, or may be in the nature of a fable. You might select stories familiar to the dominant culture in which you are presenting. For many of us, this is the overriding culture of the United States. The goose that laid the golden egg, Paul Bunyan and his blue ox, George Washington chopping down the cherry tree, and Martin Luther King's "I Have a Dream" speech are examples of this type of story. Additionally, stories in *Grimms' Fairy Tales* (2011) and biblical tales like the prodigal son can be powerful. Since they are well known, they serve as a common reference point in bringing home a point.

From this continent, Native American and First Nation stories tap rich ways of knowing; from the Middle East, Sufi stories draw from Muslim wisdom; from Asia, Zen and Buddhist themes are useful. For mythology from around the world, Joseph Campbell is the best source. Larson's (1991) *A Fire in the Mind: The Life of Joseph Campbell* is scholarly and a delightful series. Campbell urges us to find ourselves in the stories of other cultures and even from primitive mythology. Campbell's observation below was quoted by Sartore (1994).

> The comparative study of the mythologies of the world compels us to view the cultural history of mankind as a unit; for we find that such themes as the fire-theft, deluge, land of the dead, virgin birth and resurrected hero have a worldwide distribution—appearing everywhere in new combinations while remaining like the elements of a kaleidoscope, only a few and always the same. (p. 28)

You can also tell stories from a completely different cultural tradition than known by the audience. As long as you can explain the context, and it is relevant, people will learn from hearing this

TWO STORIES WORTH WATCHING

A brief example of Native American storytelling can be found on YouTube. This is the tale of two wolves living inside us and the internal struggle humans encounter between good and bad.

The Cherokee Legend of Good Versus Evil

 https://youtu.be/TzZQm4yhPns

 Follow up by watching "The REAL Story of the Two Wolves" to witness the initial wisdom, lost in the popularized version of this tale.

https://youtu.be/JHXwPFMvaXk

class of story. In fact, when selecting stories for indirect communication, these have an advantage. Because they require more effort from the conscious mind to follow the story line, the less direct messages can more freely interact subliminally. Here are some possibilities:

■ *Native Wisdom for White Minds: Daily Reflections Inspired by the Native Peoples of the World* (Schaef, 1995) is a source for reflections and prayers from Native Americans.

- *Growing up Amish* (Wagler, 2011) is a true story of one person's quest to find himself.
- *Afghan Dreams: Young Voices of Afghanistan* by Tony O'Brien. Photojournalist O'Brien and his brother-in-law Michael Sullivan interview children of all ages about their lives, their fears, and their dreams (O'Brien & Sullivan, 2008).
- *The Two Mountains: An Aztec Legend* by Eric Kimmel (2000). This Aztec tale tells of the magical relationship and marriage of the son of the sun god and the daughter of the moon goddess, a story that echoes the Biblical legend of Adam and Eve.

Trainers in Adaptive School seminars will sometimes tell this story to make it acceptable for participants to pull chairs together for a conversation. We heard it first from Carolyn McKanders, an accomplished counselor and noted trainer of Cognitive Coaching seminars and Adaptive School seminars.

WHITE PEOPLE FIRES

Years ago I used to travel from Detroit to Michigan's Upper Peninsula to present seminars in the Marquette area. This area of Michigan is unique in that there are thick white birch forests alongside Lake Superior's beautiful sandy beaches. I became friends with some wonderful local residents who took it upon themselves to try to make me—a city girl—a hiking enthusiast. They succeeded. Once we went hiking to find a particular waterfall that my friends called "church" because of its awe-inspiring effects. On the way we met a native Chippewa. He talked with us about being careful in burning fires. In this conversation he spoke of native people building small fires because the intent is to sit in circle to commune and listen to each other. He stated that he noticed that when white people build fires they build very large fires that made folks have to stand way back—disconnected from each other.

The world is awash in sources for stories. From films to literature, from family to biographies, and from histories to stories from other cultures, storytelling material abounds. I've referred to film and YouTube, but stories can be found in any kind of drama, for example, Arthur Miller's play *Death of a Salesman* (1976) or Nikos Kazantzakis's *Zorba the Greek* (2014).

The roots of many stories lie in figurative language—allegory, fable, or metaphor. It turns out that metaphor plays an oversized role in communication because the left hemisphere processes it in addition to the right, and some metaphors have very long shelf lives. Madeline Hunter, a noted educator in the latter part of the 20th century, once said, "The mind is like wet cement. The first idea it gets sticks." That's informed one of my understandings about learning for decades. Stories from cultures not your own can be particularly rewarding. Of course, as so well depicted in the play *The Music Man*, you need to know the territory—the audience—and your goals for them.

METAPHOR STORIES

A metaphor is an implicit comparison between one situation that's often poorly understood and another that's generally better understood. Some rich examples are slow as smoke off a manure pile; slower than pond water; restless as the tip of a cat's tail. One favorite of mine is Senator John McCain's comment regarding the investigation into Russian Meddling in the 2016 election: *This is a caterpillar. There are more shoes to drop.*

The most frequently used metaphors relate to something from nature that can be seen, felt, touched, or smelled, as demonstrated by the journal entry in Figure 5.1. One reason why metaphors are such a powerful means of communication is that they evoke these sensations in the brain, causing us to recreate experiences as if we *were* experiencing what was being told. Metaphor stories are yarns in which parallels exist between the listener and the fabric of the story. Because metaphor stories interact with the unconscious mind, they can be very influential in a group's thinking and behavior.

While this chapter opens a conversation about metaphor, Chapter 5 provides an extended grasp, including how it interacts with our brains. Subtexts of metaphors, the messages below awareness, are explored there.

☐   iStock.com/A-R-T-U-R

📖   iStock.com/Julichka

5

WHY ARE
METAPHORS
IMPORTANT?

Metaphors provide a glimpse into unstated perceptions of the world. They relate concepts to dissimilar ideas and are understood easily by listeners. Metaphors come with subtexts; hidden meanings that are accepted without question by the listener. "I'm *stuck in* this job" (as if activities are containers); "Why can't I *get this across* to you?" or "The president's speech *threw* the audience *into* a frenzy" (as if communication is sending). Jobs are not containers that can be entered and exited, no physical object is exchanged in a conversation, and speeches don't physically push people into anything (Landau, Meir, & Keefer, 2010). Taking the hidden meaning of subtexts literally, of course, would not make sense, but these layers of less obvious meaning influence the listener. More about subtexts is addressed later in this chapter. Worksheet 1 in the Appendix provides practice exercises to detect them.

Linguists assert that metaphor is the way the mind thinks (Lakoff & Johnson, 1980), as illustrated in the journal entry in Figure 5.1. Carter-Liggett at the Pacific Graduate School of Psychology in Palo Alto, California, theorizes that during a story, listeners experience a biochemical change detectable in the their saliva. It's related to the story's capacity to relax recipients and engage the right hemisphere of the brain, the wellspring not only of imagery but of our capacity to deal with change as well (Parkin, 2010).

Figure 5.1   Fishing: A Journal Entry

"I'm learning that I serve the group better when I can be fluid with my presentation skills and responsive to the needs of the group. It's kind of like learning to fish. At first you're out there practicing your casting technique, relying on an expert to determine what flies or bait to use, and guessing at what type of fish might be in the water. As you gain fluency, you begin to read the river, note the cut bank where a rainbow trout might hide, adjust your cast to work with the flow of the water, check your body to eliminate shadows that will spook the fish, sample the stream to see what your target is feeding on ... making decisions to answer the question, "Why am I doing this, this way?"

Mike Webb, Principal in Anchorage, Alaska

Metaphor is a form of figurative language used to describe a certain use of a word or phrase standing in for a concept. Another is *allegory*, which seems to relate more to story form. Yet the bulk of the literature on storytelling refers to the indirect or figurative tale as metaphor.

The potency of metaphor comes in part from the reactions of the motor complex of the brain. When literal sentences like "The player kicked the ball" are heard or read, the brain reacts as if it were carrying out the described actions. For sentences like "The patient kicked the habit," the brain reacts in a similar manner as it did to the literal sentence. This means a person actually experiences a simulation of the activity in the story (Bergen, 2012).

References to seeing, as well, activate the visual cortex, and so on.

HOW METAPHORS ARE PROCESSED

Language processing is generally considered a left hemisphere function for most people. But figurative language, a category that includes metaphor, involves the right hemisphere. This suggests that metaphors may be processed to some degree in both hemispheres. What is known with certainty is that listening to metaphor sends blood flowing to those parts of the brain responsible for processing kinesthetic, visual, olfactory, and auditory input. What is also known is that the left hemisphere of the brain processes language sequentially, logically, and literally while the right hemisphere processing is simultaneous, holistic, and implicative. It is as if when hearing metaphor we experience two stereos simultaneously, each tuned to a different station.

RIGHT HEMISPHERE ENGAGEMENT

In one study, medical students who were reading and writing technical passages registered the highest left hemispheric activity whereas the highest right hemispheric activity was recorded when reading Sufi stories. The Sufi stories produced the same left hemispheric activity as the technical matter *plus* a surge of involvement in the right hemisphere (Mills & Crowley, 1986/2014).

Psychologists like Carl Jung, Julian James, Milton Erickson, and Ernest Rossi believe that metaphor is the process of the subjective, unconscious mind. Linguists John Grinder and Richard Bandler conclude that metaphor evokes meaning in three different stages. Their work is based on traditional linguistic studies and on their own documentation of the work of Milton Erickson, a therapist and hypnotist who used story extensively to communicate with the unconscious mind.

The three stages are as follows:

1. The meaning of the story is literal.
2. The meaning of the story is associated with some generic or impersonal thoughts or data.
3. The meaning of the story is recovered from deep within the listener's personal experience.

It is at this last stage that metaphor is most potent. The listener may remember feeling sad at the death of a parent or feeling loss from a marriage breakup. Sometimes these recovered meanings are below the level of a person's consciousness. "Once the personal connection occurs . . . an interactive loop is established between the story and the listener's inner world by which the story is enlivened and further extended" (Mills & Crowley, 1986).

Of course, not all storytelling produces such visible effects. The anecdote, the one-liner, and the joke may evoke interest but not deeper processing. Speakers and staff developers who are working to employ more metaphor in their work frequently do so for at least four reasons.

CULTURE ALERT! MIND YOUR METAPHORS

Bill Powell, at the time headmaster at the Dar es Salaam International School in Tanzania, in an opening-of-school-year address to parents, praised the teachers for pinch-hitting for one another. (School had opened that year with less than a full complement of teachers.) Afterward, a new and very confused Japanese parent came to Bill asking, "Why do your teachers pinch and hit?" (Ochan Kusuma-Powell, personal communication, 2018)

FOUR USES OF METAPHOR

Metaphors are not always verbal but can be physical expressions of an idea, such as dance or body sculpting. They can also be concrete, such as shaking a penny inside an inflated balloon, symbolizing the trial and error required to get change going and how, once in motion, it takes on a life of its own. Metaphors can also be visual, as in cartoons or movies, or they can appear in organizing systems, such as murals or ceremonies.

Teachers and staff developers use metaphor on at least four occasions: (1) to teach new concepts, (2) to create and generate new ideas, (3) to empower or capacitate others, and (4) to guide groups in change processes. I comment on each of these here and then describe more extensively five specific ways of using metaphor to empower and support change.

TEACH CONCEPTS

Metaphoric aids are useful when the presenter wishes to teach content that is new to the learners and wants to build on their understanding of another system and transfer it to the new topic. Teachers use metaphor when they introduce a new concept by relating it to something they presume to be in the students' experience. An old Chinese story makes the point well.

THE PRINCE AND PARABLES

Someone complained to the prince that Hui Zi was always using parables. "Please forbid him, so that his meanings will be clear," the prince was asked.

The prince met with Hui Zi. "From now on," he said, "kindly talk in a straightforward manner and not in parables."

"Suppose there was a man who did not know what a catapult is," replied Hui Zi. "If he asked you what it looked like, and you told him it looked just like a catapult, would he understand what you mean?"

"Of course not," answered the prince.

Hui Zi continued, "But suppose you told him that a catapult looks something like a bow and that it is made of bamboo—wouldn't he understand you better?"

"Yes, that would be clearer," admitted the prince.

"We compare something a man does not know with something he does know in order to help him to understand it," finished Hui Zi. "If you won't let me use parables, how can I make things clear to you?" (Mills & Crowley, 2014, p. 8)

GENERATE IDEAS

Synectic exercises, in which participants are asked to list the ways in which one item is like another, are well-known devices for creating lots of new ideas about a topic. Bruce Wellman, co-author with me of *Adaptive School: A Sourcebook for Developing Collaborative Groups* and co-director of Mira Via, a publishing and professional development company, often gives groups 4 × 6 cards on which he has pasted a variety of images clipped from magazines. To prompt insights, he asks each group to pick one picture and decide in what ways it is like the topic they have been studying.

EMPOWER

Stories can help people access the emotional and cognitive resources they need when they are overwhelmed with negative feelings, trapped in egocentric or ethnocentric states, fixated in the past, or operating within a view of reality that limits choices. Stories that open up choices, present overarching perspectives, illuminate potential solutions, or build common ground assist people in getting in touch with the internal resources they need to resolve their own difficulties. The desired-state stories in this book are of this type.

GO BEYOND LOGIC

Much of our efforts at school reform are coldly analytical. We strategize, analyze, categorize. We weigh weaknesses and strengths, opportunities and threats. We list, rank, measure, disaggregate, and assess. We "TQM" (total quality manage) and otherwise alphabetize our students, programs, and improvement efforts. All these efforts are laudable, the tools are useful, and the intentions are good. But if they are used alone, without heart, we'll get what we've always gotten: improvements at a pace and a scale far too slow and far too low to serve the urgent needs of today's children preparing for tomorrow's world.

To elevate metaphorical thought to a level that is equal with analytical thought brings heart to the work. Try as we may, left-brain work does not create art. Yet neither is right-brain work alone sufficient. The power of utilizing the two-sided brain is dramatically demonstrated in accounts of creative discoveries. A good deal of both is usually required.

Metaphoric comparisons, of course, may be explicit or implied. Hearing Elvis Presley sing, "You ain't nothin' but a hound dog," we know another person is really not a canine but this is a way of talking about that person. When we express ideas the form is often metaphoric.

Be Like Captain Marvel. Metaphors are useful, at any phase in a presentation. I once opened a conference like this: I put a photo of myself at 8 years of age on the screen. After comments designed to connect with the audience, I told a story about when I was 8. I had confronted the boy who had roughed up June Scofield, a girl I was fond of and also 8. As the group could see by the image on the screen, I was small, skinny, and hardly a person who would initiate a fight. Regardless of this, I sought out the boy who had been rough on June, and before hitting him in the face I took off my Captain Marvel decoder ring so I would not cut his skin. "Where do such behaviors from a young child come from," I asked the audience. Children learn from models. At this time in the early 1940s, in addition to a few sports figures, the heroes easiest to find were comic strip heroes. My behavior had been just what Superman or Captain Marvel might have done. The story framed the topic that to locate models worthy of emulation today, we must look to educators.

Table 5.1   Using Metaphors in Presentations

Where and When to Use Metaphors in Presentations

Metaphors can be used for a variety of purposes and to evoke different responses from a group during a presentation or meeting. You can use metaphor to accelerate the learning and change process.

In the BEGINNING of the event, metaphors can be used to:

- Frame the topic and set the context for the interaction
- Capture and focus the audience's attention
- Hook the audience's mind and heart
- Create rapport (responsiveness)
- Pace and lead the group into more resourceful states of mind
- Set the group's perceptual filters for seeing in new ways

(Continued)

Table 5.1　(Continued)

In the MIDDLE of an event, metaphors can be used to:

- "Tee up" a new topic
- Bridge from one topic to another
- Create useful dissonance or discomfort
- Punctuate a key concept
- Plant seeds of potential options

At the END of an event, metaphors can be used to:

- Synthesize key learnings
- Create "open-sure" and pose direction for future reflection
- Frame experiences
- Link new options to opportunities for future practice
- Ground the event in purpose and relevance

(Suzanne Bailey, personal communication, 1991)

Some languages require higher right-brain activity than others. In Hopi, for example, words do not have fixed meanings but are understood only in relation to the entire communication. A story delivered in Hopi requires greater contextual understanding and hence more right-hemisphere engagement than the same story in English. Japanese, too, lives in the right brain.

Like a popular song, some metaphors seem to have an ongoing life span. These often make a point through tapping into our emotions. The person who throws a starfish into the sea on a beach where hundreds lie stranded, saying, "Well, I made a difference for that one," is an example of this type of story. Many of these can be found in books like *Chicken Soup for the Soul,* by Jack Canfield and Mark Hansen (1993/2001).

Everyday metaphoric expressions form unconscious patterns that create and organize the meaning of our work and lives. Several behavioral studies have demonstrated how metaphors affect thought. Describing crime as a *virus* rather than a *beast*, for example, makes people more likely to support crime-reduction programs that emphasize social reform rather than enforcement and punishment. Similarly, describing cops as peace officers, as is done in Great Britain, rather than police as we do in the United States guides people to a more positive and constructive view of police officers (Thibodeau, 2017).

Any metaphor carries unstated goals, values, beliefs, and presuppositions. Presuppositions are assumptions. The "truth" of the presupposition is taken for granted by the speaker and listener. By paying attention to the presuppositions leaders use and choosing their own words with care, presenters and leaders positively influence the thinking and feelings of others with whom they communicate.

SUBTEXTS OF METAPHOR

Any metaphor carries information below the surface that is accepted by the unconscious mind as true. The "War on Drugs," for example, carries presuppositions that there is an enemy; that war is hard, long, and expensive; that the desired state is to defeat an enemy; and that the beliefs and values include investing in war equipment and giving no quarter. Some observers note that it is this very metaphor that has resulted in more and more money being spent on drug prevention with fewer and fewer results. How about a metaphor like "healing the drug epidemic"? they ask.

Figure 5.2   Metaphor Subtexts

Metaphor 1
Leader as Parent

- Desired-State: Growth, health, protection, survival, reproduction
- Values: Care for others, modeling
- Beliefs: Caretaker, guardian, responsibility
- Presuppositions: Sacrifice, love—be loved, mom, dad

Metaphor 2
Leader as Captain

- Desired-State: Win, be the best
- Values: Be fit, be a team
- Beliefs: Hard work and practice
- Presuppositions: Follow instructions

As friend and colleague Bruce Wellman points out,
presuppositions, values, and beliefs vary for the metaphor of team
depending on what type of sport is being referenced: baseball,
football, tennis, or others.

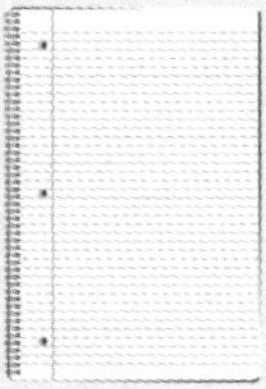

See the Appendix for a worksheet to practice detecting the subtext of certain metaphors.

Because of the brain's difficulty in distinguishing words used in either a literal or metaphoric sense (e.g., He was kicked out of school), the storyteller's language choices become important. The motor cortex is activated by either literal or metaphoric expressions. Additionally, unlike other narratives, metaphor is heard twice, once in the left hemisphere and again in the right, sending a message in stereo to listeners. Metaphor is used to teach, to ideate, and to bypass logic and is useful at many points in a presentation. The next chapter includes desirable features you will want in your stories and a seven-step strategy you can use to prepare your stories.

iStock.com/A-R-T-U-R

iStock.com/Julichka

6

DESIRABLE STORY FEATURES

TALKING TO POTATO CHIPS

A man talks to a bag of potato chips. A camera stands about 15 feet away, recording the interaction without sound. The potato chip talker is Abe Davis, a PhD candidate at MIT. He is demonstrating that everything vibrates, most of it too quickly for the human eye to discern, and that sounds can be recovered from the vibrations. So Davis speaks: "Mary had a little lamb, little lamb. . . ." The video is played back, and Davis's voice is heard: "Mary had a little lamb, little lamb . . ." and so on.

Good stories like the one above either include surprises or provide tensions that keep the audience tuned in. Davis's report in his TED Talk (2016) seems so preposterous that the full energies of our attention are riveted to the tale. This first-time intelligible human speech is recovered from silent video of an object. The proposition is so absurd that we are in his hands for the rest of his presentation. Check out his TED Talk on

this topic at www.ted.com (https://goo.gl/38H4sj).

Tension, as illustrated above, is one feature required for effective stories. This and seven other desirable features are presented in Figure 6.1.

Figure 6.1   Desirable Story Features

An engaging opening

A beginning, middle, and end

Present tense

Sensory images

Tensions

Embedded conflict

Vocal variety

Memorable closings

And finally, practiced delivery, especially at the beginning and at the ending

ENGAGING OPENINGS

Provocative starts to a story grab and hold attention. My purpose in starting this chapter with the "man talks to potato chips" was to provide a provocative entry point for readers. Provocative openings can be simple statements like "I don't have much time. I only have time to annoy you. (Pause) And that is my intention, to annoy you like a grain of sand annoys an oyster." Or "I don't want to embarrass anyone, but the persons sitting on either side of you think you know more about this topic than they do." This gets everyone engaged in laughter and therefore receptive to what comes next. Another way to make a provocative start is to begin without saying hello but just launch into a conversation or story designed to misdirect the unconscious mind. An illustration of this can be found at the beginning of Chapter 11 with the backpacking story that opened a session for a restless group of teachers during a summer seminar.

The moment audiences know a story is about to begin they enter a receptive state similar to what children do when listening to a story. Certain phrases alert groups that a story is about to be told, and adult brains scramble to activate all the neural circuits that would be active if they were actually experiencing the events in the story. "When I was seven my sister was born and my life changed forever . . ." or "On January 16th, 2018. . . ." Listeners know from these openings that a story real to the speaker is coming.

Try using the words *imagine* or *picture this* at the outset to activate parts of the brain that make internal representations. "Imagine you are at the edge of a cliff, the wind is so strong you can lean into it, below you is. . . ." On the other hand, openings that start with "Once upon a time" inform people that a make-believe story is coming and the speaker has some reason for offering it.

Another way to engage at the opening is to use a prop. Props will direct the gaze of an audience and offer another way to hook them from the first moment. A friend of mine tells a story about how he did this once in Singapore.

John was to make a keynote on the power of laughter in learning to 1,000 people following a long and boring opening by a professor. I offer this anecdote as an example of using a prop, in this case to comic effect (Garmston, 2018). When John began, the audience never knew what hit them. He reflects:

CAMERA MADE IN JAPAN

Some advance preparation was obviously required as I had to review my material and eliminate any references to North American culture with which they would not be familiar. [John is Canadian.] I also had to delete anything that was linguistically based. As it turned out the choices I made were effective.

During the break after the presentation, I felt somewhat like an aging rock star. I got a lot of attention and multiple compliments on the keynote. I definitely got off on the right foot by getting on the stage and taking a picture of the audience as the first thing I did. I got them to stand and wave and say, "Hi, Canada!" Their reaction was hilarious. Due to my own nervousness and lack of attention to my equipment, in the first couple of pictures the flash on the camera didn't go off. I looked at the camera and said, "This camera must have been made in Japan." It turned out to be good use of local humor. (J. Dyer, personal communication, 2001)

HAVE A BEGINNING, MIDDLE, AND END

Well, duh! And yet the most important aspect of this natural structure is not to be caught elaborating so long on one section that the others get short shrift. Be sure that both the beginning and end are carefully crafted. Design a turning point in a story. If the beginning was one way and the end another, there must have been a point in the middle where things changed.

Script and rehearse your openings and closings to guarantee your exact words will catch and hold attention at the start and leave the group with something memorable. You might even apply the advice I once heard given to an author: Scan what you have written and then remove the equivalent of every fifth word. The idea is offered as a metaphor to use the fewest words possible. American poet and literary critic Edgar Allan Poe advised us that in a well-crafted story, every extraneous statement, every unnecessary word, must be eliminated. Avoid unnecessary detail. No one cares if it was a Tuesday or Wednesday, so don't agonize over that—just pick a day and go with it.

USE PRESENT TENSE

While it might feel awkward to tell about an event in the past using present tense, in reality that's how most of us tell stories. "I'm in the teachers' lounge and she comes up to me and says, 'I've been wanting to tell you something about what you said yesterday.' I'm dumfounded. What is she referring to?"

USE SENSORY IMAGES

Authors and storytellers help their audience by illustrating and including verbal references to sight, sound, smell, and tactile sensations. A story with many sensory references will actually cause listeners to enter a mild trance. Chapter 8 gives information on the effects of such trances and how they come about. Here is a paragraph from an action novel in which the author uses descriptions that put you in the scene.

> *He closed his eyes. The sun was almost directly overhead. He felt the warmth on his face, heard birds off in the tree line. A breeze stirred and brought with it the scent of rosemary. For a moment, he tried not to think but just be still. (Thor, 2017, p. 93)*

To help listeners create their own experiences of a story, be artfully vague in describing a scene. In the paragraph above the author does not tell us what the birds sounded like, what the smell was like, how close or what the trees looked like. Yet we had many phrases from which we could make our own representations of feelings, sounds, images, and the man's processes.

As another example, one might say the trees were alive with color, sunlight dancing through their boughs rather than refer to the green leaves. Saying the leaves are green puts the color green in the audience's experience. Alive with color, instead, has listeners create their own colors, much richer and more engaging than you could suggest. This is not to say being sensory specific is bad—sometimes it's quite appropriate to say the ball was red. Listeners will still produce their own conception of red.

INCLUDE TENSIONS

Worry, fear, anxiety, urgency, high stakes, or conflicting goals are all examples of tension. Show these emotions by what the character does. *I pace the room with hands clasped tightly behind my back, sweat moistening my forehead.*

EMBED CONFLICT

Conflict holds our attention. The story categories identified in " Table 3.1—shift perceptions, invite learning, inspire action, seek a desired state—most likely involve some form of conflict to make a story worth telling. Story lines might regard a situation requiring compassion, solving problems such as triumph over adversity, courageously defending values, irretrievable loss, or transformation to new perspectives resulting in a changed person.

CREATE VOICES

Oral characters are presented less formally than those on the page, and you have the luxury of speaking for them. John Dyer, whom

I mentioned earlier, was skilled at creating voices on the stage. He would adopt a set of gestures associated with the person. When he put words into a person's mouth you could hear the pitch, volume, texture (nasal, throaty, quick, languid, monotone, down or upbeat), and accent, if any. John might also have a place on the stage from which this person spoke, or he could turn his body as if the person were facing him and then, to show his response, move to the position his character had just taken.

Try these ideas to increase your ability to sound like different characters. Impersonate (as best you can) some famous person or family member. Use a voice you developed in childhood—most of us have made voices for our pets, or our children before they could speak for themselves. Decide where you want this voice to be coming from—the nose, throat, chest. Do you want to portray this person as snooty, laid back, excitable? Do this at home, of course, not with a group.

USE MEMORABLE CLOSINGS

Your ending is as important as the rest of the story. Don't summarize. Don't spell out the moral of the story. Consider not providing closure. Allow room for listeners to construct what they need after the story is done.

Speakers often use *opensure* instead of closure to end a story. *Opensure* leaves a vacuum the mind wants to fill so it will continue working the puzzle after the story is over. And of course, what the listener constructs is more influential than what the speaker might tell them was said. Here are some closings I've used:

- After a story taken from an imaginary book: "So that's a great book. I think you would enjoy it."
- "And as you plan your next parent conference you may find yourself wondering which of today's insights might be applicable to the parent you are about to see."
- Following a story illustrating how one can be caught in constricting conceptions: "And for days and days and days the bear continued to pace back and forth between where the bars had been, but were no more."

More Direct Ways to Close

Occasionally one may want to be more direct and link the listeners to the storyteller's goal.

- "The reason I am telling you this is that we must not be afraid of failure. In fact, what we call failure can lead us to . . ."
- "As you reflect on what happened to Pooh, you might wonder what the affects would be if he were a member of our organization."
- "And you, like peak performers everywhere, live at the edge of your competence. And living there, you fail frequently, and when you do you fail, you fail forward."

SEVEN STEPS TO
PREPARING A NEW STORY

You've selected a story to tell. Here are seven simple steps to get the story into your mind so that it effortlessly flows to groups you meet with.

1. Make an outline of story events to aid your memory.

2. Write the story in your own words or draw a story-board or comic strip version.

3. Tell it to yourself referencing your notes.

4. Analyze your notes. Are any story elements not necessary? Edit your notes.

5. Tell the story again and again to yourself and then to a friend.

6. Retell it some more, beginning to emphasize the emotions in the story.

7. You've got the story inside you. Tell it to a group and remember to SLOW your delivery.

Winston Churchill was once reported to have given this advice to speakers: *Be brief. Be sincere. Be seated.* Poe would have loved this verbal economy. Well-formed stories are delivered in present tense (so then I say to him), tantalize us with tension, and open and close clearly and compellingly. Well-crafted stories use rich sensory vocabulary causing listeners to experience story events as if they were their own. Having a system to integrate new stories into our repertoire is helpful.

In this chapter I've tried to be both brief and sincere in describing features you want in your stories and present a tested way to develop a new story. (Thanks, Winston.) Openings are important, as are endings. Audiences appreciate an economy of words at the beginning. Groups quickly and deeply attend to your tale when this is the case. The middle part of stories often signals a transition to distinguish its function from a beginning or ending. Sensory language is captivating, a theme that reoccurs in this book. It causes listeners to reproduce, in their own neurology, the sights, sounds, and feelings the storyteller mentions. While writing this chapter I was surprised to learn that attention is not voluntary, making story elements like tension and conflict essential to capture the full attention of listeners.

You can deliver stories, of course, without being the author. The next chapter offers delivery tips.

7

DELIVERING
YOUR STORY

W hat are you like when you are most natural? Imagine you are telling a friend about something that happened to you during the day. What do you notice about yourself? If you are like most of us, you may observe that your body is relatively still, your voice relaxed, that you pause for emphasis, and periodically, the volume of your voice shifts. Depending on personality and style, you may or may not gesture while recounting your tale. While storytelling has been described as an art form, you most likely already have all the necessary ingredients in your natural speaking style.

The purpose of this chapter is to identify specific patterns, many of which you may already use, for telling a story effectively to an audience.

ANIMATION

Your body, of course, is part of the story you tell, especially because listeners are keyed into all the nonverbal information you send about yourself. Your torso, hands, eyes, facial expressions, and voice tone are important parts of the message. Sometimes you might offer a story after speaking for a while to support a concept or to make a point. At other times the story is your first interaction with the group as you rise to your feet to speak. When this is the case, stand still. Audience members are judging you when you first stand to speak, unconsciously interpreting your degrees of comfort, credibility, and competence in the multitude of nonverbal cues you send. So stand still at the beginning, so people can take your measure. After a few sentences, you are free to move.

STAND LIKE YOU ARE CREDIBLE

Experienced storytellers adopt a way of standing—a credible stance. When you are in this position, groups experience you as trustworthy and worth listening to.

Zoller and Landry (2010) observe that it is difficult for many people to change the way they stand from their default position to a credible stance. Initially it may feel contrived. Author Claudette Landry found that once she had mastered the credible stance she was able to win participants' attention and keep their focus for longer periods of time and with less effort than was required before. Zoller and Landry offer the guidance in Figure 7.1.

Figure 7.1   Five Elements of the Credible Stance

1. Feet are parallel and hip-distance apart.
2. Arms may be perpendicular to the ground, or the lower arm may be held parallel to the ground. Or both arms held parallel to the ground also constitutes a credible stance.
3. Breathe abdominally, calmly, deeply.
4. Stand still, no rocking back and forth.
5. Maintain an erect yet relaxed posture.

A few other ways of standing may communicate less reliability and are to be avoided. These include parade rest (arms down and hands joined at the back), fig leaf (arms down and hands coupled in front of the crotch), on hips (placing hands on hips), pocketing (hands in your pockets), or what I call the coach posture (crossing your arms across your chest). The most credible position is the credible stance as shown on the previous page.

Third Point

While we are on the subject of posture, one other form is worth mentioning: the third point stance. Because participants' eyes follow the storyteller's eyes, if your eyes stay focused on the group when gesturing in the distance or at an object in the room, participants will look at you and not the area you are referencing. In the third point, the storyteller directs his or her gaze toward the location being talked about.

Sound, gesture, and movement communicate your content. Gestures should be noticeable neither by their absence nor by their boldness. When speaking publicly, gestures should be above the waist but below the neck unless you are pantomiming some distressed personality. Use both hands to gesture even if you are holding notes or a prop in one of your hands. Shakespeare (2017) knew this when he had Hamlet advise the players who were to perform for the King,

> Nor do not saw the air too much with your hand, thus, but use all gently, for in the very torrent, tempest, and (as I may say) whirlwind of your passion, you must acquire and beget a temperance that may give it smoothness.

CENTERING

Figure 7.2   Be Centered

A major principle of any public performance is to appear grounded and calm. To achieve this you can monitor and adjust your oxygen level by the form of breathing you employ. When you experience stress, your breathing becomes shallow and you hold your breath for brief periods of time. The neocortex in your brain, the site of language and reasoning, needs a full supply of oxygen to function. Stress shuttles precious oxygen to the limbic system to ready the body for survival.

Diane Zimmerman and I addressed ways of dealing with this phenomenon in our book *Lemons to Lemonade: Resolving Problems in Meetings, Workshops and PLCs* (2013).

When you are centered, you become more in touch with who you are and depend less on outside approval. The centered state is simple, natural, and powerful. To center yourself:

Stand

- Allow both your arms to drop naturally to your sides.
- Spread your feet so that they are appropriately balanced beneath you.
- Take several long, deep breaths.

(Continued)

(Continued)

- With each slow exhalation, imagine the tension flowing out of your body from head to toe.
- Allow your spine to lengthen; mentally reach toward your hair and pull a strand of it up so that your neck is elongated and your spine is comfortably stretched.
- Imagine wearing a heavy overcoat causing your shoulders to relax.
- Now, from this position, sway slightly back and forth for 10 to 15 seconds, gradually decreasing the size of the sway until you reach center.
- Next, imagine that you are pushing both feet into the floor, then release that tension.

VOCAL VARIETY

Without variety, audiences may fall asleep. Fresh out of the Navy in an afternoon community college class, I remember my geology teacher for the drone with which he delivered his material. Needless to say, I slept through most of the class. I received a D and was so annoyed with myself I took the class again—from a different person—because the topic was of great interest to me. It helped, of course, that the new professor was more engaging.

Vocal variety is the mark of the accomplished speaker or story-teller. It is a combination of pitch, tone, volume, and rate.

I think of pitch as a range between high notes and low notes. While a steady pitch might be used to make a dramatic point (e.g., "He looked. He looked again. He could not believe it."), the body of speech should move up and down the scale congruently with what is being expressed. I think of tone as the emotional quality of speech. I want the feelings I am describing to be matched by a tone helping listeners relate to the feeling. Volume, of course, is how loud, how soft. Speakers sometimes drop their voice to a whisper to make a point—audiences lean in, entranced. Finally, rate is related to pace—slow, fast, medium. Like all voice quali-ties, this too needs variety.

The vocal nonverbal for credibility is the narrowing of pitch when you speak followed by the lowering of pitch at the end of a phrase. If you like, think of the Allstate car insurance commer-cials where a person speaks and suddenly a voiceover starts with a low, confident voice. (Google it and listen.) As you listen to the voiceover, just about every statement ends with a decreasing pitch (Zoller, 2012). To make your voice sound credible, just drop your chin at the end of a sentence. Your voice tone will automatically drop. You don't, of course, use this voice all the time.

INTENTIONAL MOVEMENT

When you move, consider moving strategically. As impressive as the TED Talk speakers are, I notice that some of them move within a small imaginary circle at their feet. TED speakers are advised to visualize a small area around their feet to represent their stage, and then move within that space. However, a different way of changing location enhances your story. Move to another position when giving voice to one of the characters in your story. Adopt a voice different from your own. As I tell a story about different persons I might move to my left and say, "This group was happy with the result," and then moving to my right I might say, "But this group was not." I have placed characters in different places.

 **A STORY WORTH WATCHING**

Breaking Glass—A Leadership Story by Dima Ghawi (2014)

 https://youtu.be/2nr62XUtIu0

"As a child," she begins in her inspiring story of growing into leadership. There is much to observe in this unique speech outlining a personal story of breaking out of cultural limitations to find a sense of personal and professional purpose. The speaker starts with a prop, engaging us with its novelty as we entertain a fantasy of what might happen to it during her speech. Using her prop, she is able to move with greater intention than we see with many TED speakers. See if you notice when it appears that she has forgotten her lines and how she recovers. Appreciate her nonverbals and how the physical reference to herself changes over the course of the story. My sense is that her story would have been stronger if she had closed it after asking, "What are the limitations you are living with?" See my first paragraph under "Use Memorable Closings" in Chapter 6 for my thinking.

I vividly remember Carolyn McKanders telling a story about how much she appreciated her daughters giving her a birthday card. She stood at one end of the stage as she began, "And then . . . there was Kenny." She marched silently to the other end of the stage. Once there, she displayed an image of the card her son Kenny had made for her and talked about how she needed to be understanding of her preteen son's inappropriate sense of humor in his birthday card creation. I've watched Carolyn do this a number of times, and it never fails to be effective.

Here are some general tips about physicality while telling stories. Emphasize transitions or special points in your story with visual paragraphs. To execute a visual paragraph, you make a statement, pause, break eye contact, step to another part of the room, and make the next statement. Visual paragraphs help participants tune in. This is television jargon for moving with deliberate silence to some new spot on the platform. This alerts an audience that something different is going to be said (Garmston, 2018).

Take advantage of the many natural transitions in your story to signal these changes by your position in the room:

- After your introduction and as you start the body of your story
- As you move from your first main point to your second
- As you give voice to different characters in your story

By slightly changing your voice, your position on stage, and your head movements, you can make each character come to life. The audience can now see the story as well as hear it. The energy level with which you enter the stage tells the audience about the tenor of your presentation. Take the stage with confidence. If your message is a somber one, walk soberly with a serious face.

Syntax and Vocabulary. A tip on developing style is to punch up the important words in your story through inflection, gesture, and word placement. Place the most important concept at the end of a sentence, permitting you to pause, and then emphasize that word with the appropriate inflectional stress. For example, in the sentence "We want to work together for student learning," if the important concept is "together," sequence the words like this: "And so, we work for student learning—*together*."

If, however, the most important concept is "students," you might arrange the sentence in this sequence: "And so, we work together for the learning of *students*."

As noted elsewhere, using words like *imagine* helps the audience form images about what you are saying. Jane Chen made a TED Talk about a low-cost, lifesaving incubator for premature babies in the developing world. She opened like this:

"Please close your eyes and open your hands. Now imagine what you could place in your hands: an apple, maybe your wallet. Now open your eyes. What about a life?" (Chen, 2009).

As she asked, "What about a life?" she revealed an image of a tiny baby sleeping in the palm of a pair of aged hands. The word *imagine* has a magical quality for audiences in that it prompts that very activity. Pause for 3 seconds to 5 seconds after the word to give people time for imagining. Donovan suggests you use this word to help people be a fly on the wall for your stories. "Imagine you were with me the day I first looked at my newborn's face." Or "Imagine what it would be like to be on the wing of a burning plane protected only by firefighting gear" (Donovan, 2014, p. 116).

You can use the word *imagine* at the beginning of your stories and again at the end. "Imagine what your next parent conference would be like if your first goal was to understand rather than give information." This is a form of pacing for the future, in that you are inferring that if the audience uses the principles of the story, valuable results will be produced.

USE QUESTIONS TO INVITE THE AUDIENCE IN

Ask questions that invite the audience to reflect about their lives to engage listeners. "Have you ever had an experience so awesome that you were rendered speechless?" Once you see heads nodding, the group has accessed that experience and your story can begin. "Once, when I was a firefighter/runaway/student, I had this experience." Whatever your life is about, audience members can now connect with you across what unites us—our common human experiences—not what makes us different.

Donovan (2015) lists types of questions you might ask to engage audiences:

- *Polling:* "So how many of you are sort of making yourselves smaller?"
- *Seeking confirmation:* "If you use emotions poorly in online negotiations, bad idea, right?"
- *Provoking thought*: "Can power posing for a few minutes really change your life in meaningful ways?"
- *Creating suspense:* "So I'm watching this behavior in the classroom, and what do I notice?" (p. 125)

Another way to invite an audience into the story is to place them in the scene. Consider these two openings: "I was in my office one day when . . ." or "Envision yourself in my office with me one day when. . . ." The second form brings listeners in to experience the unfolding drama with you. Incongruity in speaking kills credibility and focuses audience attention on mismatches between story content and presentation. Richard Nixon was a classic example of incongruity in speech. He would say, "I want to make three points about that," and then, as if responding to an echo in his own mind, a moment later he would display three fingers to the audience. Gesture, inflection, posture, and language congruently presented with story content are very winning.

Congruity includes matching voice quality to story content. When effective speakers talk about an exciting event, their pitch and pace increase correspondingly. When speakers describe certain feelings, such as sadness or pain, their voice may drop, becoming resonant and slow.

Congruity also means crediting story sources. An ounce of personal credibility is lost when speakers tell a very popular story in the first person. This causes audience attention to shift from the story to some unconscious considerations about the degree to which the speaker can be trusted.

In the final analysis, delivery style means freely becoming who you are. Effective speakers may initially learn by modeling someone else, but over time they increasingly let go, relax, and are just themselves with an audience. They disclose personal mistakes. They stay light. They give primary attention to maintaining rapport with the audience. Since we each have a limited amount of memory space to bring to a presentation, our content should be well integrated so we are free to concentrate all our conscious energies on monitoring and adjusting our relationship with the audience. Developing one's own presentation style is merely the process of gathering experiences and maturing in one's ability to just "be" with audiences.

Finally, a tip about language: Locate a good thesaurus. Expand your word choices to enable increasingly subtle descriptions in your story. Notice how these next words each convey a different experience: brilliant, luminous, intense, dazzling, bright, vivid. Guard against overuse of certain words. For some speakers everything is "great." For more persuasive folks there are synonyms like large, enormous, gigantic, vast, huge, massive, gargantuan, and others from which to select. Interestingly, the shorter the words, the more power they convey.

I assume that for many readers, parts of this chapter were not considered news. It's self-evident that telling a story is more than a script and words. In all the descriptions of gestures, voice, movement, and even ways to stand, it's important that each of us remain true to who we are. That's not to say we can't learn new skills. I learned the credible stance and third point gesture, for example, well into my career. They've both helped me become more effective. Perhaps more important than speaker presence is how listeners are drawn into the story to experience in-the-moment occurrences—*so I'm at the ball park and what do I see?* Inviting an audience to become part of the story is an important language skill. Ted Sloane, a poet friend of mine whom we meet later in a story about a backpacking trip, tells me the best thesauruses anywhere are those meant to support crossword puzzle aficionados. The richer your vocabulary, the greater ease you will find in developing stories for the unconscious, the topic of the next chapter.

iStock.com/A-R-T-U-R

iStock.com/Julichka

PART III

CHANGING
BEHAVIORS
WITH STORY

The Desired-State Map informs the trajectory of all stories
designed to improve attitudes and behaviors. Part III contains
examples of the map being used and introduces a fundamental
process for inviting others to change. Examples and analysis of
change-making stories are explored. Chapter 12 summarizes key
understandings in the book.

8

PROMOTE CHANGE: STORY STRUCTURE AND EXAMPLES

A story without a destination is like a sail without wind. It will lie lifeless in the minds of listeners, losing connections to its purpose and credibility for the speaker. Three examples are provided that proved instrumental in effecting change wherein thinking was informed by the Desired-State Map, described in this chapter. This chapter extends this information to describe the first act storytellers must perform to move groups to more desirable states.

Story purposes might be to entertain, provoke reflection, make a point, alter perceptions, change behaviors, teach, or establish a touchstone on which other activities can rest. The most important consideration in selecting a destination is to know the present status of the listener. As the nomadic salesman in *The Music Man* advised, "Ya gotta know the territory" (Wilson, 1957). Knowing the territory includes not only who is there, but also what emotional states, cultures, perceptions, and orientations to the event are present. In other words, what is the context? You can start your preparation by learning about the listener's existing situation.

- If an individual, what might be the person's goals, external pressures, and/or reasons for seeking change?
- If an individual, what resources might propel this person to greater satisfaction or productivity?
- If a group, what is its current context? What are its purposes, external pressures, history, and composition of its membership?
- What existing thought or behavior patterns might be counterproductive to an individual or group's purpose?
- Equally important is to imagine what values the individual or group holds, what beliefs and principles drive their hard work on behalf of students.

DESIRED STATE

Whatever stories you find or craft must acknowledge the positive intentions of the group. Once you have an understanding of the territory it's time to ask yourself: If this is the existing state these folks are in, what desired state might free them to access

Figure 8.1   Desired-State Map

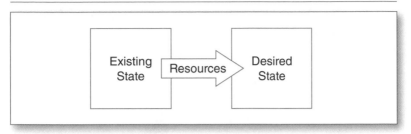

their knowledge and skills in service of their goals? This takes you to the purpose of telling a story: What outcome do you wish to achieve?

To learn about the context in which you will be speaking, inquire about the listeners' emotional states. What dynamics might be happening within the group? Are there issues about which the individual or group feels strongly? What frustrations might be present?

Resistance persists when resisted.

RESISTANCE

Friend and colleague Kendall Zoller recognizes that when resistance exists within a person or a group, the best way to strengthen the resistance is to fight back against it (personal correspondence, August 2016). Imagine two figures standing, arms extended and palms facing one another. One is resisting, the other is pushing back. No progress is made in either direction. But have the one resisting cease that behavior, simply walk backward a few steps, and inquire about the issue as the resister sees it, resistance is gone, and greater chances exist for resolution.

When Kendall senses resistance, his approach is to acknowledge it as a healthy function when addressing certain challenges. He explores the three categories in Table 8.1.

Table 8.1   Acknowledging Resistance

1. What are the emotions people may be experiencing about the content or event?	2. What are the reasons people are experiencing those emotions?	3. What do they value and believe that brings them to work?

Looking through these lenses provides empathic insights into the current condition. People's behaviors are rarely ill-intentioned but emerge to protect or serve them. Such responses are more likely to be instinctive rather than deliberately selected. Thus, a compassionate understanding of their internal states is necessary to craft a story that metaphorically describes their existing state in a recognizable way. Kendall cautions that this process is about data collecting; it is not what you believe, it is what the group feels and why.

Stories that help listeners move toward desired states and change behaviors can be delivered to individuals or groups. What follows are three examples, one generic and two for special circumstances. The first story, told to graduate students, can be used to invite paradigm shifts about doing things the way they've always been done. The final two stories were designed for special situations: one to proactively shape positive behavior for a group during a meeting, and the last to help an individual improve personal performance.

APPLYING THE DESIRED-STATE MAP: THREE EXAMPLES

1. Shouting at a Parent

> *The first time I witnessed the application of the desired state was through a hole in the wall of my principal's office in Marin County. Because I was studying to be a*
>
> *(Continued)*

(Continued)

principal he would periodically invite me to peek at some interaction from which I could learn. On this day, an Air Force officer and parent was seated in Ross's office. From my vantage point, I could see him clearly. His voice was raised, and all of a sudden his fist swept from over his head to pound on Ross's desk. Clearly, Ross sensed the existing state was far less than desirable. Ross responded in kind, with his own fist slamming the desk, and in a voice that started loud but tapered off to a conversational tone. At the end he said, "You're at the end of your rope with this teacher, and if we were to sit and talk this out I believe we can get a solution." The officer nearly melted into his chair, and from then on the two had a normal conversation.

Ross matched the energy and anger in the officer's voice with his own, then gradually decelerated until he was at a conversational level. In other words, Ross chose a response that let the officer know he was totally understood (existing state), which contributed to an understanding between the two men. This (the resource) was necessary to move to a desired state, which Ross did by modeling tone and language at the end of his statement.

It's important to recognize that Ross was in control of himself throughout the entire interaction. He feigned anger to connect on an emotional level with the officer. Later we look at Ross's behavior through another lens—that of pacing the officer's anger, then leading him to a more reasoned state.

2. Bear in the Cage

Teachers use stories to invite novel ways of considering a situation and help listeners later recall important concepts. In the following example, a group of graduate students had been asked to design and implement a field project that broke with the long-established tradition of setting an objective, doing linear planning, and implementing the plan in an ordered, sequential manner. Instead, they were required to lead teachers in a school improvement project where the leader had no predetermined solution in mind.

The problem these graduate students encountered was that after 17 or 18 years of formal schooling, their thinking was so locked into a linear problem-solving approach that they experienced enormous difficulty breaking away from those mental bonds to consider the project in a fresh way. The professor told the following story:

Not long ago, the San Diego Zoo acquired a new bear. Zoo officials were proud of this and hastened to install it in the delightful natural environment the zoo provides for its large animals. The bears are kept in an area from which visitors walking along a street can see them. There is a very low wire fence that reaches to people's waists. Beyond that is a very deep moat, and beyond that is the environment for the bears. In that space there is typically a large pool of water in which a bear can rest, dip, swim, and cool itself. Beyond that is a cave into which the bear can retreat for privacy and sleep, and to the left of this area, in full view

(Continued)

(Continued)

of the visitors, are several trees on which the bear can sharpen its claws or scratch its back.

To their dismay, when the animal caretakers received the bear in its traveling cage, they realized that this attractive environment had not yet been built. They decided that the kindest thing they could do would be to put the bear, still in its travelling cage, into the center of its new home while workers completed the setting.

On the first day, having been sedated for travel, the bear awoke, stretched, stood unsteadily, discovered that the movement of the cage had stopped and began to pace slowly at first, to the right perimeter of the cage and then to the left. At each end of the cage, it rose up on its hind legs and roared. Back and forth the bear paced. The managers, seeing the apparent distress of the bear, ordered the workers to hurry so that the bear could be released as quickly as possible to its natural environment. The workers did so. And as they worked, the bear continued to pace. Two days went by, 3 days, 4 days; the bear continued to pace in its cage. The manager, by this time becoming alarmed by the habituated behavior of the bear, ordered the workers on double time. Nearly around the clock the workers labored, until finally, on the 6th day, the environment was complete.

The next day, once again sedated so the managers could remove the bars of the cage from around the bear, the bear awoke in its new environment. The bear stretched, stood unsteadily, and looked around. Now, with no bars between itself and its new home, the bear could see a large pool of water. Beyond that was an inviting cave, and off to the left was a pair of trees, sturdy and strong.

The bear turned to its right, took three steps, and, where the bars of the cage had formerly been, rose up on its hind legs and emitted a long and anguished roar. The bear dropped, turned, retreated to the other side where the bars had been, rose up and roared, and in this manner continued to pace back and forth in the narrow confines of its previous cage.

Later, over the course of the semester, when students were mired in old ways of thinking about their projects, the professor referred to the "bear cage." Students were helped to step beyond their own mental restrictions.

TO TELL THE BEAR IN THE CAGE STORY WITH MAXIMUM EFFECT

Place masking tape to represent cage boundaries. Stand within these imaginary cage walls, lift your arms, and roar and pace within the designated area. Pantomime the bear waking from sleep, rub your eyes, and again pace within the original space, roaring and raising your arms at each edge.

Later, when you wish to reinforce the concept, walk into the space designated for the cage. Your mere presence there will remind students of the story.

3. A Strong, Yet Delicate Rose

I was hired once by a superintendent to help his assistant superintendent for instruction become more effective with the educational community. The superintendent sat behind his desk while the assistant superintendent and I sat facing him. His message was blunt. Sophia (not her real name) was going to be fired unless she established more positive relations with the community. Bob was here to help. Did she want his assistance? Her response was yes.

Through a couple of coaching sessions it became clear that Sophia was a highly motivated, detail-oriented, organized, and driven individual. However, she lacked social sensitivity. My job was to help her see herself through the client's eyes and determine what she could work on to improve her relationships. It was clear that her professional knowledge base was strong, as was her command of processes within the organization, but she was perceived as cold, remote, and a taskmaster lacking empathy. It was not in her demeanor to be soft.

We began by describing the existing state (Figure 8.1) from the community's perspective, then moved to construct a desired state in which Sophia would have the respect of the community. This brought us to what she had to do to make this happen. After one or two sessions this became the context for a story.

By now I had enough rapport with Sophia that she accepted my suggestion that I had a story for her that might improve her situation and that for the story to be maximally effective it was important that she be totally relaxed. "Would it be okay," I asked, "for me to lead you through some relaxation exercises?" She agreed. Relaxed, breathing deeply and naturally with closed eyes, she listened to this story.

One night as you are preparing for bed, you notice a single rose not previously in your awareness. It's nesting near your bed in a simple vase. Deeply relaxed, you enjoy the rose and feel a deep comfort, when for some reason, you become aware that you are dreaming, as perhaps you have dreamt before but probably not of a rose like this.

You are sensitive; deeply sensitive of ways the rose is becoming even more precious to you in the deepest parts of your being. More and more deeply you are being drawn to its comforting fragrances and the tenderly delicate textures of its colorful petals. From time to time as you are gazing gratefully at the rose, thoughts of unease arise, concerns of possible vulnerabilities for the flower. It is an unpredictable world, you know, one in which the rose is not in control of situations in her environment. You wonder how this delicate spirit could be safe from unexpected dangers.

Your eyes slip downward from the soft petals near her crest, and you encounter on her strong green stem a thorn. Your gaze continues to move down, down, down the stem to encounter another thorn and another, each sharper, bolder, and stronger than the others. You realize the rose has dual strengths, the capacity to please and defend, flatter and protect. Wondering about this, you fall into an even deeper sleep. When you wake, you wake refreshed and energized.

"How do you feel?" I asked. After a quiet moment, she simply said, "I feel at peace."

In the following weeks reports began coming in to the superintendent that clients were inviting Sophia to meetings, listening to her ideas, returning her phone calls, and interacting with her pleasantly, which had not been so in the past. Sophia, in many ways like the rose petals, began to show her softness. She showed her consideration and respect for the community. She began listening to its members, became facilitative rather than demanding in meetings, and of prime importance, she listened and invited opinions.

PRESUME POSITIVE INTENTIONS

Knowing the territory means deeply sensing your listeners—their circumstances, reasons for emotions, and what they value. Fighting resistance is a losing proposition—to resist strengthens it. Skilled storytelling is compassionate, recognizing that even problematic behaviors are positively intentioned. They are simply ways listeners have chosen to take care of themselves—even if sometimes ill-advised or wrongheaded.

In the communities of Cognitive Coaching and Adaptive Schools we refer to our understanding of these self-care motivations as presuming positive intentions. Behaviors are driven by intentions, and at the base of these intentions is the desire to take care of oneself. I am often the first beneficiary of this presumption because it frees me from judgment, blame, or defensiveness, all conditions that reduce my ability to think clearly in the moment.

That resisting resistance causes persistence is an important reality. The Desired-State Map uses this principle because it does not linger on an existing state but focuses first on a desired state and the resources necessary to reach it.

While the three examples in this chapter are different, the stories of Ross, the bear, and Sophie all have similar components essential for their success. The next chapter addresses how the first step in each example is to get in tune with the situation, as it exists. This essential but counterintuitive move is described in detail.

iStock.com/A-R-T-U-R

iStock.com/Julichka

9

MEET GROUPS
WHERE THEY ARE

As your eyes continue reading the words on this page, from time to time you may become aware of the thoughts in your mind, or the sensations in your hand or down there on the soles of your feet, or awareness that you are starting a new chapter . . .

Communications that pace the experience of listeners are feedback loops. They essentially feed back the emotions or attitudes occurring for the majority of group members. They do so nonjudgmentally, acknowledging, in the listeners' minds, the legitimacy of what they are experiencing. This is common in all successful relationships and is the essence of rapport—I see you and accept you as you are. In situations in which a group is overwhelmed or angry, suspicious or blaming, pacing their experience is essential to helping them achieve a more productive state. This is the concept we explored earlier relating to resistance. To guarantee that the group's experience remains stuck or even worsens, try to talk them out of it. Push against the unproductive emotions and they only strengthen.

The sentence at the beginning of the paragraph is my attempt to report (pace) the experience readers may be having as they begin this chapter. Communications to pace simply reflect what is there. They add nothing new. Their major purpose is to establish connection, acknowledge nonjudgmentally what is there, and establish rapport with a group.

In storytelling, as in other leadership roles, pacing is used to assist a group in developing alternative attitudes, points of view, or behaviors more positive than the group currently experiences. Acknowledging a group's current state is a necessary step toward helping them acquire a more responsive emotional state.

PACING

When audiences are at their best, we establish rapport and enter into their world, making it easier for them to understand what we are communicating. Joseph O'Connor and John Seymour (1990) describe this as pacing, or building a bridge between the learners' experience and yours. Entering their world allows greater permission for you to invite them into yours. This happens naturally when all is well.

When tensions exist within an audience, pacing requires acuity in interpreting the inner state of an audience as a whole. This allows the speaker's statements to be regarded as accurately describing the state of most audience members. So the presenter provides two story lines within a tale, one for the conscious mind to follow, another to send messages to the unconscious. The purpose of telling an interesting story for the conscious mind is to bypass the filters that might block difficult or uncomfortable information from coming in. Listeners may have the experience of wondering, "Why is he telling me this?" which occupies the conscious mind, leaving less energy for defensive filters to work.

Long before I knew about storytelling I began a session with what appeared to be a hostile school staff. With scowls and crossed arms they seemed to be saying, "We dare you to try to teach us." Rattled, I knew I was in trouble, and the only thing I knew to do was get them active. I had them brainstorm the worst and best things that could happen today while I recorded. Then, pointing at the worst things chart, I said, "If any of these things happen, let's have a collective groan." Fortunately, this broke up the resistance. In hindsight, I realized I had paced their attitudes in the charting.

Pacing Tips

When making comments about an audience, be artfully vague to allow the maximum amount of people to associate with what is being said. "Many of you," "Some of you," and "A few of you" are some examples.

> "The people had many special skills and certain interests," "some degree of hope existed," and "she breathed deeply as she moved into the fresh clean air" are examples of language vague enough to suggest a theme but, like a radio drama, allow the listeners to make their own picture.

INDIRECT SUGGESTIONS

Direct suggestions are usually resisted. But suggestions embedded in a story prompt the association and reorganization of ideas, understandings, and memories. The listeners may unconsciously accept these suggestions as long as they are congruent with their best intentions.

The legendary therapist Milton Erickson (1966) paced the client's in-the-moment experience as part of his pattern to induce trance.

> *As your eyes continue reading the words on this page while you're looking at it, from time to time you may become aware of the thoughts in your mind or those sensations in your hand or down there on the soles of your feet . . .*

Because such statements are verifiable in one's experience (I am reading the words on the page), they allow the therapist or storyteller to insert an embedded suggestion (you may become aware of the thoughts in your mind, etc.). By describing what is going on in the mind of the listener, the storyteller is suggesting that what is being said is true. Therefore new statements, not in the listener's experience, might also be accepted as true.

"Stories to pace and lead" or "desired-state stories," the topics of Chapters 10 and 11, are intended to bring listeners to greater resourcefulness. These tales acknowledge and validate existing emotional states and/or points of view to lead to states in which participants are capable of making new choices.

Pacing is the first part of a two-phase strategy for leading a group to a more resourceful state. Situations that call for desired-state stories are settings in which a group is resistant, apathetic, blaming others, angry, or even exhibiting behaviors that detract from the effectiveness of an otherwise sound presentation. All these presumed negatives can be transformed by a carefully designed desired-state story. I use the word *presumed* negatively because such behaviors are usually ill-informed ways of protecting oneself.

Figure 9.1 describes what recipients to a pace may experience. The goal of pacing is to activate the following responses.

WHAT LISTENERS EXPERIENCE

People listening to a desired-state story may experience:

1. My feelings and behavior are considered normal in this situation.

2. Because the speaker names thoughts and feelings I have not directly expressed, I feel a connection to him or her; the speaker understands me. (Johari's Window)

3. At levels below conscious awareness, conditions for change are being set.

   a. A nonjudgmental acceptance of my current state

   b. A glimpse of a possible desired state

   c. Permission to move toward this desired state without feeling bad about myself

A pace precedes a lead. Leads are described in detail in Chapters 10 and 11. Here is an overview of what listeners experience during the lead.

Figure 9.1   Pacing and Leading With Storytelling

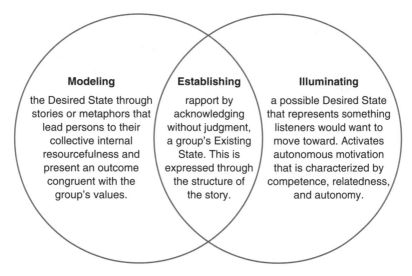

Modeling
the Desired State through stories or metaphors that lead persons to their collective internal resourcefulness and present an outcome congruent with the group's values.

Establishing
rapport by acknowledging without judgment, a group's Existing State. This is expressed through the structure of the story.

Illuminating
a possible Desired State that represents something listeners would want to move toward. Activates autonomous motivation that is characterized by competence, relatedness, and autonomy.

Source: James Roussin

1. I feel connected to my own resources for taking care of myself.

2. Autonomous motivation has been activated, allowing me to discern and select behaviors different from those I am using now.

3. I have a desired state I can move toward. This may be occurring at levels below conscious awareness.

Sometimes, as in the following situation, the pace-and-lead story can be about oneself, which appears in the form of a conversation. In this example, a principal learned she was being reassigned to a new, low-income, overcrowded school on the other side of town that was being formed from a school being closed. It was April, and she was told she had to manage both schools until the end of the school year. People were very upset. Teachers (as well as parents and students) did not want the school closure to occur; they were disturbed by their powerlessness and at the way the closing had taken place. They were also apprehensive about leaving the familiar and moving to a new school. The receiving community wasn't any happier. The following scene took place just after the decision to create the new school had been announced. About 50 unhappy people were crammed into the library after school to meet the new principal. Some were sitting on the carpeted floor. The atmosphere was tense.

AN EXEMPLAR: PRINCIPAL GONZALES

Hello. My name is Camila Gonzales, and I'm the principal at Pippin School across town. I've just been assigned as your new principal. I don't mind telling you that I don't want to be here. I feel dumped on. [At this point she paused and scanned the attentive faces in the room as people held their breath.] *Let me tell you why. I'm now at a school where the staff and I have a good working relationship. We are like family; we care for one another and enjoy working hard together for the students. I know the students and parents, and we all know what to expect of each other. Things are working well, and together we're doing a good job.*

Now the district has told me that I need to come over here and manage this new school. Furthermore, I have to start now to begin putting it together while I am still responsible for the school I'm currently serving. I don't mind telling you that I'm upset, resentful, and I don't want to be here [long pause]. *I guess our job is to see what we can do to make the best transition possible.*

The principal's language paced the traumatic experience of each staff member. Silence followed her opening comments, during which teachers reflected on their own experience and where the principal's comments had led them—"what we can do to make the best transition possible." She also used language like "family" and "we care for one another and enjoy working hard together for the students," inferring that this type of relationship will be possible with this new situation. Griping and resistance were absent that day. Grieving was at a minimum, because the principal and teachers suspended it for this meeting to work productively together to identify practical next steps.

Had the principal tried to say that the people there were upset, she would have been setting herself up as an outsider telling the audience what they felt. If they perceived her as an outsider, group members would have evaluated her comments. But by describing her feelings, being open and vulnerable, she was able to pull the group in.

Pacing has been reintroduced here as a preface to the next chapter, which offers a set of linguistic tools instrumental in deliberately communicating with the intuitive mind. It is a special art, almost a Rogerian way of working with groups, in which whatever is going on within the group is accepted as the audience's best known way of dealing with their situation.

Chapter 10 introduces the concept of two minds operating in each person and the relationship to the linguistic skills involved in speaking to the unconscious, or intuitive mind.

10

DESIGN FOR THE
INTUITIVE MIND

The unconscious is always listening.

Milton Erickson

BREAK THE POT

Last night, I was talking with a gardener. I asked her how she knew when to repot a plant. "When it shows signs of lifelessness," she replied. "What are some of those signs?" I asked. She explained that the leaves turn brown or brittle

(Continued)

(Continued)

and that the roots may force their way out of the bottom of the pot. "So what do you do?" I asked. "Well, first I break the pot," she said. "Break it? That sounds so violent. Why do you do that?"

"Well, consider the options," she said. "If I tried to pull the plant out of the pot it has grown too large for, it might go into shock. But if I break the pot, then I can gently and lovingly remove the plant from its shattered pot and place it in a larger one, where there will be enough soil and nutrients for it to grow.

I stared silently at the audience for a long, discomforting moment. Then I said, "Our purpose here today is to . . ."

This was my opening with a faculty assembled for a full day to hear the results of sensing interviews in which they expressed anger at the principal and complained about each other. What brought the group to this perilously uncomfortable point were such severe complaints about the principal that the board decreed she would be fired if she did not straighten things out by the end of the school year. It was May. When I completed my introductory remarks—I had not even introduced myself—I walked directly to a posted agenda and stated the purpose of the meeting. The group appeared stunned.

INVOKING RECEPTIVITY

Audience members wondered what on earth a broken pot had to do with this session. To make any sense of my opening statement they needed to search their personal experiences for some sort of match to a gardener breaking a pot. This search is at the same time conscious and intuitive, subliminal and instinctual. Winner of the National Academy of Sciences Best Book Award in 2012, Daniel Kahnerman's *Thinking Fast and Slow* (2011) offered a metaphor for two inherent functions of the mind. System 2 is our slow, deliberate, analytical, and effortful mode of reasoning, and System 1 is our fast, automatic, intuitive, and largely unconscious mode. It is System 1 that creates a rough draft of reality and the system to which metaphor speaks. System 2 draws on the impressions of System 1 to arrive at explicit beliefs and reasoned choices.

To make sense of my opening statement, audience members needed to use both systems to search their personal experiences for connections. Unlike most searches, this is not a quest for exact or literal matches but a hunt for possible meanings without which an incoming communication cannot be made any sense of whatsoever. This search is compelling, automatic, and largely unconscious. It is a state of internal focus and processing, inducing a sort of reverie or everyday trance. This is called a transderivational search in psychology and cybernetics.

David Gordon (2017) describes what must have been a transderivational experience with a friend.

The Peugeot Confusion. In most cars to lock a door you push a button down. To lock the door in Gordon's Peugeot, the button must be pulled. A friend began the process of getting in the car, saw the button was in the up position, and "with the confidence of thousands of experiences with car doors" proclaimed the door to be broken. He was so sure of his analysis that even though the window was open, he never once tried pushing the button down.

Gordon uses this example to illustrate how a set model of reality, while helpful and frequently time saving, can also be a disadvantage. Set models are relatively inflexible and limiting, offering few choices when confronted with difficult issues. The story illustrates the tremendous power such models have on our thinking. Finally (after Gordon's help), the friend had to sift through his experiences with automobile doors, retrieve his world model, and reassess it to make sense of the anomaly.

The search conducted by Gordon's friend was energy intensive, and both System 1 and System 2 had to be engaged. *Trans* refers to across, beyond, through, or changing, as in transfer, translate, transport, transfigure. *Derive* means to receive or obtain from an origin or source, often from reasoning or inference. Therefore *derivational* refers to retrieving from several origins or sources such as memories, personal experiences, work events, mental models, intuitions, values, and/or beliefs. This is demanding internal work, requiring an intense focus on internal landscapes. The search is always personal because there can be many meanings to the speaker's words.

Figure 10.1   Transderivational Searches

Trans	Derivational	Search
(Across)	(Derivations)	(Hunt)
To hunt across various derivations.		

BEYOND WAKING AWARENESS

Trance denotes any state of consciousness other than normal waking consciousness. The rhythmic songs of soldiers marching, the melodically soothing voice of a storyteller, meditation, prayer, or a repetitious activity like drumming induce trance states. You enter a state of trance when you drive a long distance and start to feel disassociated from your body and the car. Milton Erickson (1966), a renowned psychiatrist and psychologist specializing in hypnosis and family therapy, held that trance was a common everyday occurrence. When waiting for a bus, or reading, or doing strenuous exercise, it is normal to become immersed in the activity, focus internally, and go into a trance. Many definitions of hypnosis describe it simply as being suggestible while in trance.

An example of pain management through hypnosis is found in a famous Erickson case. Erickson masterfully used embedded suggestions to treat the cancer pain of a patient named "Joe." Joe, a retired farmer turned florist who did not believe in hypnosis, had been given a month to live. Facial cancer had eaten away much of his face and neck and caused intolerable pain. Medications were not very effective. Yet Erickson's two conversations with Joe relieved Joe's pain. He lived in comfort for 3 months after his first meeting with Erickson (Henley, 2015).

Erickson explained that despite his "absurdly amateurish rhapsody" about a tomato plant, the metaphor he used to talk about Joe's pain, Joe had an intense desire for comfort and to be free from pain. This meant that Joe "would have a compelling need to try to find something of value to him in the author's babbling," which could be received without his realizing it (Erickson, 1966, p. 207).

Hypnosis: A state of highly focused attention or concentration often associated with heightened suggestibility and relaxation.

STORY ELEMENTS FOR
SUBLIMINAL PROCESSES

Contrary to public understanding, a trance is merely a state of intense concentration. When stories are of sufficient interest and contain parts of the elements shown in Figure 10.2, listeners concentrate intensely, develop personal meanings, and may be influenced by indirect suggestions within the story. This pattern is enriched, as any storyteller knows, by referencing the five senses within the story, often in a nonspecific way: "rich colors," "familiar fragrances," "soothing sounds," "a riot of color," or "aromas associated with family."

Figure 10.2   Story Elements for the Intuitive Mind

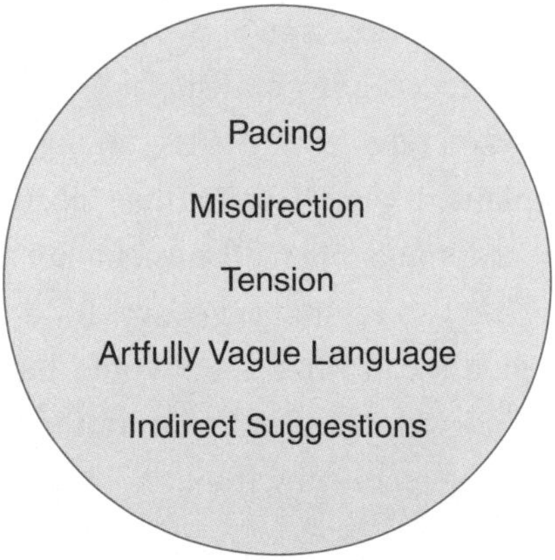

Pacing

Misdirection

Tension

Artfully Vague Language

Indirect Suggestions

PACING

Pacing, as is explored in Chapter 9, is the first in a two-step pacing and leading process used to support groups in moving to more resourceful states (Costa & Garmston, 2016). With stories come transformative narratives, stories that encourage listeners to move beyond their current states into more productive ones. One way to think about pacing is linking what you say to the experiences of the audience as if metaphorically walking alongside them. This is a way of acknowledging the validity of the listener's subjective experience. Without starting where a person is in the moment, it's awfully hard to lead him or her to more productive states. Pacing is essential when your goal is to support groups.

MISDIRECTION

Whenever we feel confused by what we hear, we naturally attempt to make sense of the communication. To do this, we must go inside; for a moment we may miss the next few words in the story as we search for the meaning of what we've heard. The search takes us within our own experiences, understandings, and memories to construct meaning. A storyteller is like a tailor providing the cloth to the listeners, who measure and sew their own clothes. Misdirection launches this search for personal meaning.

Forms of misdirection include conversational openings, pre-suppositions, double binds, and metaphor.

Conversational Openings

Examples include *"Last night, I was talking with a gardener . . ."* found at the beginning of the chapter. I started this sentence without preamble or even introducing myself. Additionally, gardening was not the topic of the day; listeners had not yet connected to this event. Erickson's work provides another example. His initial comment to Joe was, *"Joe, I would like to talk to you. I know you are a florist, that you grow flowers, and I grew up on a farm in Wisconsin and I liked growing flowers. I still do"* (Henley, 2015).

Presuppositions

Presuppositions are ideas assumed in a sentence. Listeners tend to accept and even mentally act on them, making them part of how they are experiencing the world. "As you think about your successes . . ." "As experienced teachers . . ." "As folks seeking truth . . ." "As you might wonder about learning even more . . ."

Double Binds

Examples include *"Don't obey these instructions"* or *"You are free to do as the curriculum guide dictates."* Double binds either contain conflicting messages as above or presume choice where either choice leads to the same outcome. When parents of a young child say, *"Do you prefer to have your bath before or after dinner?"* they are using a double bind. Erickson might say, *"I don't know whether you will make this change immediately or within the next week."*

Table 10.1   Presupposition Examples

Coaching Language	How the Mind Responds
As you consider options	This phrase sends the mind scrambling to sort out options, likely creating some that had not previously been available.
At times when you experienced success	The mind searches for previous successes and in doing so accesses the sense of efficacy felt at those times as well as memories of how they successfully mentally approached challenges.
As an experienced educator	"As" indicates it is me being described, and I equate skills and attainment with "experienced."

Metaphor

With the faculty described in the opening of this chapter I used the metaphor of a broken pot to describe what would be happening in the session. In Chapter 11 you will see the description of a backpacking trip used as a metaphor to describe the experience of a seminar group, and you will find an expert visiting a tiny planet used as a metaphor for my work with an elementary school staff. You can say things about a group you are with through metaphor that you would never be able to say directly.

ARTFULLY VAGUE LANGUAGE

When communication lacks detail the listener must fill in the detail from his or her own experience. I may say "Christmas tree" and have in mind the decorated trees of my youth with silver, blue, and red globes against a backdrop of tinsel thrown over green branches. The listener, however, can't intuit all the detail I am imagining so recovers a picture of a Christmas tree of his or her experience. Nonspecific nouns, verbs, and nominalizations are forms of imprecise language.

These vague descriptors allow listeners to create representations in their mind that relate to their experiences. "<u>People</u> say this group is dedicated to <u>high standards</u>." Notice that both underlined terms in the sentence can be interpreted in a variety of ways. "Which people" and "what is a high standard" are not defined. The next sentence contains a presupposition and vague language: "Because we both want Rafael to <u>succeed</u>. ..." Mutual desire for Rafael's success is being presupposed. What is meant by "succeed"?

Nominalizations

The term "nominalize" comes from linguistics. It is, in effect, converting a verb or adjective into a noun, or naming processes as if they were things—as in "love," "friendship," "trust," or "communication." "Trust" is not a thing one can put in a pocket, but rather is a process, or series of processes, in which "trusting" is occurring—a series of behaviors people associate with trust. A value to storytellers is that because a nominalized word is artfully vague, the listener cannot sit outside as an observer but must become part of the story as he or she makes unique mental representations understandable to him or her.

TENSIONS

Stories that begin with paradoxical or nonsensical premises produce tension and engage left brain and right brain, the left processing the language and the slightly slower right brain connecting with the nonverbal creative and emotive elements. On the surface, my story of a gardener and broken pots had nothing to do with why people were in the room, and thus engaged minds in trying to make connections. The connections I had in mind were that this was going to be a rough journey, there were probably going be some shocks along the way, but it was all happening in the spirit of loving repair. This unconscious and automatic state of internal focus and processing is an involuntary activity in which listeners connect bridges between the story and their own experiences.

INDIRECT SUGGESTIONS

Direct suggestions are usually resisted. But suggestions embedded in a story prompt the association and reorganization of ideas, understandings, and memories. The listeners may unconsciously accept these suggestions as long as they are congruent with their best intentions.

As noted in the beginning of this chapter, the unconscious is always listening. We can facilitate listeners' access to it with a number of linguistic nuances. Paradoxes, artfully vague language, and misdirected beginnings all invite the listener to work at processing what is being heard. Erickson's work with treating pain testifies to the remarkable and difficult-to-comprehend reality that messages to the unconscious can actually remove pain, as it did for his patient. As Erickson talked, Joe's unconscious searched (transderivationally) for meanings he could apply to his personal situation.

Two terms were demystified in this chapter: trance, a fairly ordinary state we fall into under many circumstances; and hypnosis, a condition of intense focus in which the mind is vulnerable to suggestions. Five skills were identified for speaking to the intuitive mind: pacing, which was described in the last chapter; misdirection; vague language; tension; and indirect suggestions.

In the next chapter guidelines for constructing a pace and lead story are described. Two stories that changed the behaviors of two different groups illustrate this.

11

HOW TWO STORIES CHANGED BEHAVIORS

—————————————

This chapter describes stories told to two different groups
that in each case changed the groups' behavior. They are
desired-state stories that primarily utilize pacing and leading, a process described in Chapter 9. Three levels are described:
(1) the general conditions for a well-formed story, (2) the special
features required for a desired-state story, and (3) the unconscious
processing of the story stimulated by transderivational search.

Consider the search for meanings that audience members
might have made when I began my 3-day presentation to high

school teachers. Eighty teachers had signed up for a 10-day summer professional development program. I was to teach the last 3 days. An assistant superintendent called me the night before I was to speak to warn me that over the last 3 days many teachers in the group had become rude, disinterested, and disruptive. I asked him why. He confessed that the speaker during that period was lecturing on designing classroom activities and was extremely boring. Even though his message was about student activities, all he did was talk and show slides.

I began my presentation with the following story.

THIRD MAN OUT

Good morning. I imagine some of you are thinking that signing up for this program was a good idea at the time, but now you're not so sure. In any event, I hope that, like me, you have a good summer behind you. This year I went backpacking in the Sierras with my buddy Ted, as I often do. But on this trip he invited another hiker, which changed everything.

Here is what happened. Ted called. "Do you want to go to Red Can Lake this year? We could go north through Yellow Hammer Canyon and then up to the ridge overlooking the lake." Excited, I said, "Sure!" Then began the process of selecting gear and arranging where to meet. We both like to travel light so I packed, repacked, and repacked some more. At the trailhead a few days later, I did a final sorting of my pack, hefted it onto my shoulders [pantomiming this] *and started up the initial climb. I had forgotten the feel of the weight on my back and the torture in my legs going up that first rise. Maybe this wasn't such a good idea after all, I thought. At the top, we sat, leaned our backpacks and selves against a tree, and rested. From that point on, it began to be pleasurable. There are always difficult spots, but getting into the rhythm of walking, smelling the forest aromas, and feeling the occasional cool breezes became pleasing. As we made it to the top of successive hills, I sometimes paused, taking in the valleys, mountains, and cloudless blue sky as far as the eyes could see.*

Several days along the trail, Ted's friend joined us. For some reason, with him there, the trip began to lose some of its attractiveness. Sometimes I became bored. Sometimes I found I was irritated by the changed dynamics. But we trudged on with no option now to abort the trip; we were too far in to quit. I found myself kicking rocks off the trail and sometimes lagging behind to throw stones into the creeks of cold, clear running water that we crossed. I became disinterested in the conversations even though Ted's friend had a lot of good information. Looking back, trying to figure out why I had lost interest, I had to be honest; Ted's friend was

(Continued)

(Continued)

just boring. Then, about 6 days into the trek, Ted's friend departed on a different trail.

The next rise we took opened to a better view. We were now so high, it seemed like I could actually feel the silence in the still air. The soft sunlight on the distant mountains gave me a sense of satisfaction. I became aware of the play of light and shadow on forms around us. I also began to notice the sounds of pocket gophers scurrying across the granite and could hear the calls of nearby birds. From this point on time seemed endless; we continued to trek, enjoying our surroundings.

The final 3 days with teachers went well. Members were focused and engaged, and no behavioral difficulties arose. One teacher came to me at a morning break to exclaim he hadn't noticed so much time had passed, a suggestion embedded in the story.

This backpacking story illustrates pacing the experience of an audience when their feelings are running deep and strong enough to torpedo the objectives of the meeting. Should a group see a workshop as irrelevant and feel angry or frustrated at having to be there, the real attention in the room is subterranean; energies are below the surface, diverting power and direction from the stated purpose of the meeting. When such feelings permeate a group, the presenter starts with a story that paces, then leads the group to more desirable states. The anatomy of the backpacking story is further described in the Appendix. Later in this chapter we examine the architecture of a pace-and-lead story. Now, let's delve into the conditions for effective stories.

GENERAL COMPONENTS OF
A WELL-FORMED STORY

Chapter 6 describes features desirable for a good story, including engaging openings, using present tense, employing sensory images, and utilizing tension and conflict. Figure 11.1 adds further conditions to this list.

Figure 11.1   General Conditions for a Well-Formed Story

- Factual specificity that activates internal representations
- Presentation congruity
- Audience appropriate; relates to topics or experiences within the audience's familiarity
- Elicits empathy
- Contains moral or point that remains somewhat submerged
- Creates internal representations that are "trusted" by the unconscious mind as credible or real

FACTUAL SPECIFICITY

Verifiable data increases the listener's confidence in a story. "It was December 7, 1941. Gerry's mother was to give birth that day but had no idea what was happening." Specific dates, especially when they can be checked or in this case are widely known, verify the authenticity of the tale. When listeners get a set of specific facts or thoughts that match their experiences or understandings, a connection occurs and the story becomes relevant on an emotional as well as intellectual level.

PRESENTATION CONGRUITY

Matching the storyteller's face, voice, gestures, and demeanor to the unfolding events of the story creates a seamless connection of audience to story. Incongruities prompt the listener to become an observer when story and delivery don't match.

AUDIENCE APPROPRIATENESS

Educators easily connect with stories about students, parents, or teachers, just as football players relate to stories about sports. However, relevance to job title is just a small portion of what might be appropriate. The larger connections are emotional— stories of challenge, of achievement, of empathy, and the full range of emotions and values.

ELICITS EMPATHY

As noted earlier, humanistic stories naturally evoke empathy, create neurological changes, and awaken a desire to help others.

CONTAINS SUBMERGED MORAL OR POINT OF VIEW

"The moral of this story is" almost always inhibits listeners. Stories invite listeners to make their own meaning. It is the meanings created by the listeners that have the greatest potential to be acted on.

CREATES INTERNAL REPRESENTATIONS

When audience members create an image, sound, or feeling in their mind, prompted by sensory language in a story, those internal representations are trusted as "true" because they emerge out of personal experiences and mental models.

Previously we examined the structure of pacing and the anatomy of leading. Here are additional elements of a pace-and-lead story.

Figure 11.2   Conditions of Desired-State Stories

Bypasses protective filters

Parallels the audience's situation

Lingers on point(s) of irresolution, internal conflicts, or discomfort

Marks embedded commands

Offers resolutions

BYPASSES PROTECTIVE FILTERS

Adults learn by relating, comparing, and contrasting new information with previous concepts, data, and experiences. Critical to this process is receiving new information. However, information that challenges deeply held beliefs often has the effect of stacking a wall of defensive logs between the listener and the new ideas. These structures can be erected so quickly that no "sunlight," or new idea, has a chance to get through them. Sometimes a presenter's most critical job is just to get the information heard. In these cases, effective speakers will shine material right past the defensive logs of the listener's beliefs by aiming for the cracks, through which the sunshine of fresh data can flow. Two approaches are used to do this. In the first, the speaker suggests a process for receiving discordant information, perhaps through anecdotes.

How many of you saw the movie Spiderman*? How about* Independence Day*?* Star Wars*?* Wonder Woman*? You may notice that when you see these kinds of films, you leave your beliefs outside the theater door. And when you come out of the theater, they are still there. You simply pick them up again, and they continue to be yours. While watching* Superman*, for example, you probably suspended your belief that a man can't fly. You did that so that you could enjoy the film. If you had watched the film while filtering all the scenes through your belief that people can't fly, your attention would have focused on the mismatch between what you believe and what the film portrayed. All around you, people would be enjoying the movie, but you wouldn't be having any fun.*

I suggest that today you use this same strategy of briefly suspending your beliefs, because the information I am going to present may be new, counterintuitive, or very different than what you have been taught before. You may wish to do this first, before taking on new information so that you can then compare it to your existing information and experiences. I invite you to put your skepticism on hold and put your beliefs in your pocket or in a filing cabinet, knowing that you will retrieve them later to compare them with the new information you'll get here.

PARALLELS THE AUDIENCE'S SITUATION

Another device that speakers use to get past defensive filters is to tell a story that parallels the dynamics in the problematic situation but does so at such a distance that audience members are not threatened. Helen E. Buckley's (1961) vivid poem "The Little Boy" is one example of this. In the poem, Buckley addresses ways of teaching children that keep them overly dependent on the teacher. She depicts a child's first teacher as over-directing a class of children drawing pictures. The boy, in an initial art experience, starts to make a beautiful pink, orange, and blue flower with his crayons. The teacher corrects him, showing how to make a red flower with a green stem. While he liked his own flower much better than the teacher's, he did not say this, but just turned his paper over and made a flower like the teacher's—red with the green stem. The boy's early schooling continues like this with his teacher until he is transferred to another school. On the very first day at his new school, the teacher says, "We are going to make a picture."

The following story illustrates the final two attributes of a pace-and-lead story, lingering irresolution and embedded suggestions.

Tension is a deliberate and necessary part of this story. In this case the tension offered to the listeners is the non-resolution. The expert in this story cannot figure out what is happening. "He knows something is the same for what both groups of plants are communicating, yet something is somehow different."

While this story was being told, the teachers' faces were like children's: open, quiet, examining, deeply attentive, knowing full well that I was talking about them. But somehow, in story format, this is permissible.

LINGERS ON POINTS OF IRRESOLUTION

Points of irresolution, conflicts, and discomfort create a tension in which the listener unconsciously grapples with ambiguity or uncertainty. In The How Green Is My Garden story below, the storyteller says, "Puzzled, he ponders on the distinctions in what he is hearing," inserting a tension necessary for a pace-and-lead story in which listeners will arrive at their own realization of what is happening.

THE HOW GREEN IS MY GARDEN STORY

Hi, I'm Bob Garmston. My job today is to give a summary of what you said in the interviews and help you start planning around whatever problems you'd like to solve. Before I start, though, I'm curious if any of you have read the new children's book How Green Is My Garden? [Blank faces, because the book did not, in fact, exist.] *Well, let me tell you a little bit about it, because you might enjoy it. It's in a Dr. Seuss format, with wonderful pictures. It's about a gardener who lives on a very small planet, and he asks an expert from another planet to come and examine his gardening to see how well he's doing. So the expert comes in, carrying a clipboard, and interviews each of the plants. As he does this, he discovers a very puzzling phenomenon: All the plants have essentially the same data, but they are reporting it in very different ways. He can't quite make out what the distinction seems to be. For example, he talks to some of the plants and they say to him* [I adopt a whiny, falsetto voice], *"I don't like it when the gardener waters because he floods my roots and they get all soggy and it's damp and uncomfortable, and he's a very inconsiderate gardener." The expert talks with some other plants, and they report the same data but describe it differently.* (EMBEDDED SUGGESTION) [I shift to a logical, rational tone.] *"You know, I don't like it when the gardener waters, because frequently he leaves the hose unattended, water begins to flood my roots, it gets very damp and uncomfortable, and I need to let him know that. So sometimes I yell, Hey, up there! Back off with the water, will ya?"*

As the expert continues to interview the plants, he gets similar data reported in these different ways. Puzzled, he ponders on the distinctions in what he is hearing. (LINGERING IRRESOLUTION) *Finally, he realizes that what is happening is that some of the plants are just complaining, while others are stating the difficulty but taking responsibility for talking to the gardener about it in a way that makes improvement possible.*

MARKS EMBEDDED COMMANDS

Earlier indirect suggestions were described as statements made in conjunction with verifiable comments about a client's experience. You have probably used some of these common phrases in your conversations with others. They are, in fact, indirect suggestions for how listeners should think, feel, or act: "You probably already know. . . ," "You may. . . ," "Sooner or later. . . ," "Can you imagine. . . ," or "You might not have noticed. . . ."

Erickson called these indirect suggestions "commands," in keeping with his role as therapist. In the context of storytelling

I prefer to think of them as embedded options in that they open up positive choices for the listener to make. The storyteller, through what are essentially positive presuppositions, thus creates a generative space in which the listener can be self-directed and productive.

The last phrase in the story below, "talking to the gardener about it in a way that makes improvement possible," is an example of an embedded command. In fact, these members of an elementary staff did just that—they were constructive in their comments, a behavior not previously typical of them. In normal speech, these directives might come in the form of a comment attributed to someone else, "A lot of people say. . . ," or a question, "Don't you agree?" Because the brain cannot process the absence of a concept, the message is "You agree." Parents often learn that "Don't spill that . . ." often has the opposite effect. Embedded commands are often marked by changes in tone, volume, gestures, or facial expressions.

As a therapist Milton Erickson was known for using story extensively to communicate with the unconscious mind. In the following excerpt he sends continuous messages suggesting comfort to a man suffering extreme pain not controlled by medications. The words in italics are his embedded commands. "*You know, Joe* . . . I like to think a tomato plant *can know the fullness of comfort*, . . . *one day at a time, each day*. . . . A tomato flower slowly opening, giving *one a sense of peace*. . . , *one can feel such infinite comfort* just knowing this" (Haley, 1993, p. 301).

OFFERS RESOLUTIONS

Sometimes a story allows you to say things to a group that you may not have permission to say directly. In the following situation, confidential sensing interviews had been conducted with an elementary school staff. Each person had been asked to describe the strengths and problems of the school and to make recommendations. After the interviews were completed, the group met to have the data presented to them. The purpose of the meeting was to identify the major problem(s) that the group wished to address and to start a problem-solving process. Just before meeting with this staff, I learned that a few teachers in the group were consistently negative, complained bitterly, blamed the principal, did not take responsibility, and usually derailed staff efforts to resolve problems. Because of this, I began the session with this story.

Listening to a storyteller can promote innovative problem solving and foster a shared understanding regarding future ambitions (Denning, 2000). The listener can then activate knowledge and imagine new possibilities. Together a storyteller's tale and the listener's mental processes can create new solutions (Denning, 2000). The teachers in this meeting were incredibly responsive on this day. They took full responsibility for the data that was presented. They engaged productively and rationally, identifying problems to work on and possible resolutions.

It turns out that stories converse more directly with the listener's memories, emotions, values, and even the unconscious mind than figures, data, case studies, or reports could ever hope to achieve. Stories touch us internally, providing information that in other forms would be blocked from our reception. Because of this, stories not only entertain and teach but also persuade. In this chapter are examples of stories to overcome difficulties groups can encounter before sessions even begin. Figure 11.2 reveals conditions that are necessary for stories to be effective. Each story opens in such a way as to bypass defensive filters. *Third Man Out* parallels the audience's situation, lingers on points of irresolution, marks commands, and offers solutions in suggesting an acceptable desired state.

Chapter 12 attempts a synthesis of major ideas from the previous 11 chapters. Following that and before the Appendix is a catalog of goal-directed stories organized in the four categories addressed in the book and shown below.

SHIFT PERCEPTIONS	INVITE LEARNING	INSPIRE ACTION	SEEK A DESIRED STATE
These stories invite listeners to move beyond current frames of reference, to entertain new ways of observing and interpreting their worlds.	These tales offer learning opportunities about presentation skills, courage, and internal processes.	This set of stories inspires, encourages, and reveals how leaders influence those about them.	These stories illustrate ways presenters and leaders lead others to more productive states, attitudes, and behaviors than what currently exists.

IN CONCLUSION

Storytelling has reached a new level of consciousness for leaders in many fields. It's become clear that stories persuade far more effectively than facts. Correspondingly, leaders lead more effectively when they polish their storytelling skills and increase the use of stories in their work. Whether a workshop presenter, principal, coach, curriculum expert, superintendent, CEO, or advertiser, your messages penetrate listeners' minds through stories.

Neuroscience tells us why. Stories cause chemical changes in the blood, which in turn evoke empathy, cooperation, and desires to serve others. Unlike other forms of talking, they are processed in both hemispheres of the brain, allowing the reproduction of sensations and images as we listen. Certain forms of language in stories cause listeners to reenact the experience in their heads, seeing, tasting, hearing, and feeling what is being told. Ideas in stories feel as if the listener has generated them, and these ideas tend to be implemented. In contrast, advice and suggestions have a poor record of use.

A central premise in this book is that stories persuade and invite changes of perception. They can be catalysts for learning, prompt action, and even be instrumental in improving difficult situations. This premise is held in a higher context, that each person is responsible for their experiences and actions. One goal of leadership is that people act in accordance with this principle to embrace and use their personal and collective responsibilities.

Knowing the general attributes of a good story allows readers insights with which to select—and refine, if necessary—stories from other sources as well as design their own. Stories designed to improve behaviors have additional elements, including misdirection, pacing, artfully vague language, and embedded suggestions or commands. Spoken stories are not ready to present before polishing. This includes rehearsals sufficient to make the story one's own, then attending to the skills of an exceptional presenter. A leader's voice, movements, dramatization, and even manner of standing help a story come to life. Ways of developing personal experiences into leadership stories and locating story material from other sources are offered.

Stories, of course, are not the property of one culture. Because cultures throughout the world have created stories within the contexts of their civilizations, borrowing from other groups requires providing context. Storytelling is as ancient as the origin of humans living in groups, because the brain, even in antiquity, has a need to make meaning of events and circumstances. As precious as food, humans need to know the meanings in their lives.

Very few 75 cent words are used in the book. One important exception is the word *transderivational*, the unconscious internal processes one enacts when hearing a story. It is through this search for personal connections to story elements that a story becomes transformational.

Perhaps not so well-known yet important practicalities of storytelling are elucidated. Simple stories are best; eliminate unnecessary detail and add credibility with verifiable facts. Phrases in common use are ignored by the brain (rough day) and therefore do not stimulate internal representations of the story. Particular phrasing *"And those thoughts you had yesterday . . ."* is impossible for the mind not to process. To make sense of the subject of the sentence, the brain must search internally for thoughts that it had yesterday. Adult groups enter a state much like children listening to a story, in which a light trance ensues, allowing images and ideas to penetrate. We get so engrossed, even when reading a story, that we mentally fill in the blanks should some occur. Bypassing defensive filters is essential if a story is to persuade.

Two kinds of special stories can reside within the four story purposes in the book. One is the signature story, a story about unique and enduring qualities you possess that make this your identity. This is who you are, what you are about, your values and goals. This finely crafted story can be told more than once in different settings, often in conferences or within speeches (see https://youtu.be/Zkb-zg4JCLk). Organization or work culture stories support the endurance of values within a group. In one example, the letter of a third grader is repeatedly shown to parent gatherings and new hires.

You are invited to enjoy and experiment with the 41 stories identified in the Guide to Story Locations.

STORY CATALOG

I was conducting a seminar for educators in Sacramento. A woman approached me and asked if I was the Mr. Garmston who had taught in the Twin Hills School in the late 1950s. I confessed that I was. "My husband was in your fifth-grade class," she said. "He told me you were a fabulous teacher." "Well, thanks," I responded. "But what did he know? He was only 10 years old."

I offer this as a reminder that we influence people on a regular basis and often do not learn of the gifts others have received from us. The following brief stories in the catalog illustrate some ways we influence, or are influenced by, others. They appear under these headings: Shifting Perceptions, Inviting Learning, Inspiring Action, and Seeking Desired States. Stories encountered in the book are not reproduced here.

ORGANIZING THE STORIES

Classification is always challenging. For the stories in this book I've organized each into the category of best fit. Often a story can be used for more than one purpose, sometimes with tweaking. Readers will determine purposes and forums for which they might use these stories.

Many phenomena exist outside our understanding. The first story in this section is, in a way, coming to know what we don't know. Oliver Sacks (1998) is a great source for stories related to the functioning of the unconscious. So is Jay Haley's book *Uncommon Therapy* (1993).

SHIFTING PERCEPTIONS

THE ALIEN HAND

What do we know about the unconscious mind? A more inclusive statement might be, what don't we know? Consider the following, a piece heard on NPR.

A woman suffering from epilepsy after years of almost daily seizures agreed to brain surgery. When she awoke with her surgeon in the room, she noticed her speech was a little garbled. After a bit, one of her hands began unbuttoning her blouse. Both she and the surgeon were stunned. Then the hand became more aggressive, tearing at the buttons. Neither she nor the doctor understood what was happening.

When she was dismissed from the hospital this independent hand, seemingly with a mind of its own, would periodically slap her. Sometimes the slaps were so strong a bruise was left on her face. This continued for some time and was extremely distressing. The woman, trying to understand what was happening, began to notice there seemed to be a moral reason for the slaps, as if they were trying to make her a better person. If she were to light a cigarette, the hand would stub it out. If she swore, the hand would slap her. The doctor informed her that during the surgery the corpus callosum had been severed. This is the area in which the right hemisphere and left hemisphere communicate.

She now assumes that the slapping comes from lessons taught in childhood, and whenever she violates one of those lessons, the hand slaps her.

What is really happening here? One model of human functioning presumes that what people do or say has origins in experiences that inform beliefs, values, mental models, and autobiographical identity (Garmston & Wellman, 1999). Three planes exist: the *surface structure*, where all behavior is observable; below that the *deep structure*, where mental models inform all behavior; and below that, the *reference structure*, where unique and intense initial experiences give rise to most likely unconscious mental models.

Biologically it is known that two brain hemispheres exist, each responsible for different bodily functions and skills. In most people, the left side of the brain contains the person's language functions. The right side contributes to a number of functions, such as attention, memory, reasoning, and problem solving (all of which contribute to effective communication). It is known that damage to the right hemisphere of the brain may lead to disruption of these cognitive processes, resulting in unique cognitive and communication problems.

Given human biology and the deep to surface model, a possible explanation for the plight of the woman with epilepsy might be that severing the connections between the two hemispheres of her brain caused a blurring of hemispheric responsibilities and allowed involuntary access to deep and reference structure content. A more pragmatic approach to reaching the unconscious is telling stories.

OMAR THE SQUIRREL

To know a thing you have to trust what you know, and all that you know, and as far as you know in whatever direction your knowing drags you. I once had a pet pine squirrel named Omar who lived in the cotton secret and springy dark of our old green davenport; Omar knew that davenport; he knew from the Inside what I only sat on from the Out, and trusted his knowledge to keep from being squashed by my ignorance. He survived until a red plaid blanket—spread to camouflage the worn-out Outside— confused him so he lost his faith in his familiarity with the In. Instead of trying to incorporate a plaid exterior into the scheme of his world he moved to the rainspout at the back of the house and was drowned in the first fall shower, probably still blaming that blanket: damn this world that just won't hold still for us! Damn it anyway!

–Ken Kesey (1977)

In 2004, Carolyn McKanders and I designed and facilitated a 2-day workshop to support a staff through dramatic changes: a new principal, a third of the staff to go, a larger student body, and a host of new teachers (Garmston, 2004). Omar's situation was parallel to theirs and had we known about Omar at the time we might have started by telling his story. As early as 1980 William Bridges (1980, 1991) began informing us that it is not change that is difficult; rather, it is our emotional reaction to change. A premise of this book is that to lead, through story or by any means, one must seek to understand the subjective experience of others. This is a valuable lesson we learn from the story of Omar the Squirrel. The best leaders are listeners. This is the first attribute essential to the selection and telling of stories that persuade.

LEARNING TO FORGIVE

It was a sunny afternoon. The backyard lawn was recently mowed, and the smell of fresh grass was in the air. This is California, and the sky was predictably blue over Milpitas, near San Jose in the San Francisco Bay area. At the time, my second wife Mary and my adopted son Kevin lived with me. I was 43. In a seminar I had recently heard the idea that when you were a child your parents' life was not about you.

So while sitting with closed eyes on that fresh lawn in my back yard and openness of mind, I began an internal conversation with my mother. "Mom," I asked, "how was it for you when I was a child?" I was stunned by what followed. In a matter-of-fact voice, she said, "You know, I never did want to have children." Astonishingly, those nine words, in
(Continued)

(Continued)

that very moment, released me! Released me from thinking that her pushing me away was about me. Released me from thinking the cause of my abandonment was me. Released me from my belief that the reason I was sent away was because I was the cause of her nervous breakdowns. Released me from thinking her dissatisfaction with my accomplishments was me. I suddenly had a glimmer of understanding, of her—and of myself.

What I didn't realize until years later was that the rejection was still there—it just didn't matter anymore.

CONTEXTUAL EMPATHY

On the webbed space between the phlebotomist's thumb and pointer finger, an unrecognizable faded blue and green tattoo caught my eye. "When did you get this?" I asked.

"A long time ago," was her reply. I offered that I put some tattoos on my hands when I was 15. She smiled, and her entire demeanor opened up. "Yes," she said, "I was 16 when this went on. We used ink and a straight pin to put it on."

"Yeah," I said, "that's exactly the process we used. India ink and a pin, punch-punch-punch." I mimed thrusting the pin repeatedly into the skin. "I had a buddy put 'Healdsburg High School' on this shoulder. Can you believe that? I had it covered over in the Navy."

"Yeah, I have one up here, too," she said, pointing near her right shoulder but up higher near the ridge of her back. "This one"—pointing to her hand again—"covers up the boyfriend's name that I put on there when I was 16."

We both laughed. "Decisions we make," I said.

"You know, sometimes when someone comes in to get their blood drawn from me, they see the tattoos and tell me I am evil."

I expressed surprise.

"Yeah! One person said any dirtball that puts a tattoo on another dirtball is not worth spit. A couple people have walked out, saying I'm not having my blood drawn by some-one with tattoos."

We talked about understanding how people can have attitudes, but that they would express them so rudely was beyond comprehension.

"You know," she said, "I had a 90-year-old woman come in for her second blood test. And when she arrived she pointed to her upper back and said excitedly, "Look, I got a tattoo here since seeing you."

The Powells (2009) describe three kinds of empathy: emotional empathy in which we witness the suffering of another and feel some of their pain, cognitive empathy in which we work to understand the thinking of another, and contextual empathy in which we project ourselves into the situation the other person is in and try to imagine what they are feeling.

My experience with the phlebotomist depended initially on contextual empathy. It is not necessary to have similar experiences or cultural background for this form of empathy; however, it helps.

INVITING LEARNING

SUPERINTENDENT IN SHOCK

I had organized a weekend retreat for teachers, parents, and administrators to do planning for a district-wide ESEA Title I program. Two board members were in attendance. Friday night, the superintendent rose, gave an inspirational speech about the value of many voices contributing to the shape of the program, about how he looked forward to learning from the perspective of the people assembled, and how the thinking of this group would inform the ultimate plan for the district. Loren's presentation was well received.

The balance of the weekend was spent in small-group conversation on specific questions. Each small group had diverse membership, with parents and educators in different roles. Groups would deliberate for 90 minutes, then new groups would form with new diversely engineered membership. Energy and enthusiasm remained high that Friday evening, all day Saturday and Saturday evening, and again on Sunday morning. There was a sense of efficacy and productivity through the membership, and we went into the Sunday lunch period feeling high. The superintendent rose to make a summarizing statement. Expectations were high. I anticipated that he would summarize key directions that we had heard throughout the weekend and acknowledge people for their ideas and participation. Instead, he stood and began to repeat the same opening speech he had made Friday evening. We were stunned. The group was silent.

After a few moments I interrupted and asked if I could continue the summary, which I did. Later I privately asked him what the hell was going on. He told me that just before speaking, the two board members had approached him and told him that the principal of a school had been inappropriately touching seventh- and eighth-grade children in the cloakroom. Some of the children were the board members' daughters.

It became clear to me that Loren was in shock. I explain this to seminar groups when I tell this story. He couldn't think straight. His neocortex had actually shut down as he emotionally tried to cope with this shocking information. At this point I editorialize on how we never know the full context or reasons for a person's behavior. We can never know what is in another person's head. This is particularly true for leaders, who are often bound by rules of confidentiality. But we can assume, whatever has happened, that the leader had positive intentions. This protects us from stress and enables us to stay resourceful. As long as we are blaming, second-guessing, or chastising, we cannot stay emotionally stable enough to work intelligently.

THE MINDFUL MONK

The following is a true story, reported by the man who experienced it.

A young man sought to become a monk. One day, several years into his training, a senior at the monastery disciplined him for a minor infraction. He was directed to mow

(Continued)

(Continued)

the lawn with a pair of scissors. He was incensed at this nonsensical task and was overwhelmed with a storm of anger raging within him. For a full hour, he dutifully remained engaged but also enraged, sending angry thoughts to the one responsible for his misery. His blood pressure surged, his distress took the form of angry utterances to himself. Suddenly, as if waking from a dream, he started laughing. He became aware that his agony was self-made. Rather than being present in the moment, he was reliving the interaction with the senior and keeping alight the flames of resentment he felt. Now clear that what had passed was not the issue, but what was in the present, he continued his work but found it much more pleasurable.

STUDENT TEACHER

Gary was 5 foot 10. His neat suit and colorful tie coordinated; his shoes shined. In his mid-20s, his baby-fat face was pleasant. His eyes darted nervously, and he spoke quickly in clipped sentences while his hands fidgeted with a paper clip.

I had watched him teach a critical thinking lesson in social studies to my fifth graders. His lesson plan was reasonably complete on paper; it included all the steps. He knew what to say and do, yet for some reason these fifth-grade boys and girls, normally attentive when I taught them, were playing with Gary—purposely getting him to birdwalk, distracting him and each other. Not much was learned about distinguishing fact and opinion in that lesson.

I thought more about teaching in the year Gary was my student teacher than I had in my prior 5 years of teaching experience, and thus became more conscious of what I had intuitively known before. I watched Gary puzzling over what was going wrong, analyzing his behaviors and their effects on students. Before the lesson, we talked about his intentions, his planning, and his strategies. After the lesson we talked again about which strategies worked and which did not. We searched for subtle clues in student behaviors that could indicate glimmers of achievement. We probed for the rationale guiding his spontaneous decisions about classroom interaction. Without a doubt Gary served more as my teacher that year than I served him.

CRAMMING CONTENT

By far the worst presentation I ever made was when I tried to cram into a 1-day session what I had planned for a day and a half. Weather and transportation problems had caused us to lose a half day of seminar time, and to "make it up" to this group, I spoke rapid fire, topic after topic, relentlessly "giving them full value." Even though the pain on the faces of that audience still haunts me, occasionally I find myself pressing to cover content without giving participants time to process the data. Even when I've not lost presentation time, the seeds for this mistake are frequently

(Continued)

(Continued)

in the planning stage, where my enthusiasm for what is to be conveyed overrides my good sense about the process and time needed to convey the material. The audience's interaction with the content—if learning is the goal—is always more important than the content itself.

INSPIRING ACTION

CHOOSING A PROFESSION

Taking a break from junior college after the Navy, I worked for a while for the Press Democrat *in Santa Rosa, visiting schools and talking with fourth- through sixth-grade kids. I told them that if they were able to sell their folks a subscription to the newspaper they would earn a nifty set of steak knives. One principal, Howard Rolfe, would not let me in his school. Instead he stood in the hallway explaining why he would not turn his classrooms into a commercial enterprise and telling me what he was trying to accomplish in his school. I was thrilled with his vision and passion and knew without a doubt that I would return to school and study to be a teacher.*

A Novel Supervision Gambit

Gary Whitley (personal communication, 2017) told me this story about an experience when he was assistant superintendent at Kenai Peninsula Borough School District in Alaska.

The alternative school principal was required to submit a compliance grant report every quarter of the school year to continue funding. The end of the year had arrived and no paperwork had been submitted. The grants coordinator had tried unsuccessfully to procure a report for the entire year. The deadline for the end-of-year report was in 1 week. Typically, involving an assistant superintendent for collecting a routine report was rare. However, the magnitude of noncompliance represented $1.5 million in federal grant funds.

The grants coordinator told me that her e-mail and phone calls had been ignored by the principal and secretary for almost 9 months. She was understandably nervous about risking the loss of federal funds and had made several personal visits to the school to assist with the compliance reports. Each visit ended in frustration because the principal had indicated he had better things to do with his time.

The principal earned his nickname, Brother Love, for tireless work assisting students who were not successful in traditional high school settings. The school was a lifeline for students who had challenges such as homelessness, pregnancy, or substance abuse. I was Brother Love's supervisor and a steadfast supporter of the school and its mission. However, there are limits to levels of support one can offer when blatant noncompliance risks significant funding. Brother Love, as he was fondly called, had drawn a line in the sand and was not going to submit a report. When our phone conversation reached the point that I was hoping we would avoid, Brother Love informed me: "I am all about relationships, and I am not about paperwork."

(Continued)

(Continued)

My philosophy of supervision has some room for creative insubordination. However, responding to blatant noncompliance is not a comfortable place to be with a valued colleague and friend. I decided not to respond immediately on the phone. I reminded myself that compliance is important; however, I placed more value on effectiveness and commitment to young adults. I asked myself: What is a measured response that might produce a desired outcome? I decided that I had humor and the ability to pester on my side so I dug in for a 3-day frontal assault on the problematic thinking of "I am not about paperwork." The report was due in 1 week and there were 40 other schools experiencing the end of the year and related energy that demands my attention.

I decided to call the school multiple times a day and ask for Brother Love without identifying myself as the assistant superintendent. I recorded the song "Brother Love's Travelling Salvation Show" by Neil Diamond and played it each time Principal Brother Love answered the phone.

I would hang up the phone without speaking. Noon the second day brought an epiphany for "Principal Brother Love. He called and accused me of playing Brother Love's Travelling Salvation Show" on the phone. He confided that it was distracting and could be viewed as harassment. I informed him it was actually pestering, but if I started calling his home and playing the song it might be construed as harassment.

We reached a settlement with the immediate grant reporting requirements and with interactions between colleagues in the future. The grants coordinator had all the reports on her desk by noon the next day. Brother Love and

> *I agreed that moving forward in a positive manner would mean not placing the grants coordinator or me in a situation by forcing a showdown over paperwork compliance. I valued his service and commitment to school and community. Our colleagues also have work to complete and need to be valued as well.*

In reflecting on this situation, Gary says he might have considered playing the supervisor compliance card and lost an opportunity to teach an important lesson. In a complex world we cannot dribble just one ball at a time; we need to juggle two or three simultaneously. An intense commitment and desire to serve students is a wonderful thing. Developing tunnel vision, however, even when inspired by a mission to serve students in need at the expense of other legitimate expectations, can create an environment for conflict. Helping a colleague learn to juggle by using a sense of humor communicates two important messages: (1) We need to reframe the way we think about complex work without a confrontation, and (2) I recognize the work you do is important and appreciated.

WHAT TO WEAR

My first year of teaching was as an intern at a rural school in a somewhat conservative community. Howard Rolf, the principal, and I stood in the teacher's lounge one afternoon, and he brought up the question of dress. I wore

(Continued)

(Continued)

open-necked collars when teaching and had done so through all my student teaching assignments. He told me that while many community members were used to male teachers wearing ties, this was a professional decision each teacher must make. One advantage of ties, he said, is that if you look like what people are expecting, they will scrutinize you less closely.

TAKING A STAND

Doug, age 23, began his first year of teaching elementary school in a rural community in Northern California. In the pre-service days before school began, the principal, also in his first year of administration, told teachers that classroom desks should be arranged in rows to facilitate cleaning. Distressed by this directive, Doug shared this information with a college advisor who counseled him to be clear with the principal that he was in charge of the instructional program and that furniture arrangement would serve the instructional design and not the cleaning staff.

On the opening day of school, the principal greeted Doug outside the building and asked if his desks were in rows. This is the first-time teacher, trembling with anger and apprehension, requested the two of them retreat to the office to discuss this. Still distressed, the young teacher explained his position: He was the one responsible for learning, the environment contributed to that, and as such he must be in charge of desk arrangements. The conversation ended with the principal agreeing to his stance and Doug agreeing to have the kids put the desks in rows at the end of the day to make it easier for the custodian to clean. But during the day, the desks would serve the instructional purposes at hand.

SEEKING DESIRED STATES

These stories illustrate ways presenters and leaders lead others to more productive states, attitudes, and behaviors than what currently exists. The following desired-state stories are in the book and not reproduced here. Wetting the Bed No More, The Neat Freak, Shouting at a Parent, Strong But Delicate Rose, Principal Gonzales, How Green Is My Garden, Third Man Out, and Break the Pot.

BASEBALL TO IMPROVE, NOT WIN

My fifth-grade class, like most, had kids who could hit, catch, and run pretty well and those who couldn't. Some recent research suggests that in many cases the skilled kids were a few months older than the others when entering school and as such a little more developed. As a consequence they were picked to play more often, and playing, of course, can improve skills.

I initiated a form of baseball I'd heard about because I thought it was a good idea, but was blown away at the sociological effect it had on the kids in my class. Here is the format: Team A is in the field. Team B is at bat. Team B stays

(Continued)

(Continued)

at bat during the entire physical education period. Team A groans when they learn this. But for Team A, anytime a batter has completed his or her turn at the bat, everyone in the field rotates positions. So the person playing second base moves to first, the person at first moves to the pitcher's mound, and so on. In the field the left fielder would come in to take the third-base spot and so on.

In playing baseball to win, the most talented kids take the positions of pitcher, catcher, first base, and so on. As a result, they get better and better and better, while the kid in left field (this was often me) lollygags on the grass with only an occasional play requiring his action. This kid gets no chance to improve.

So in my class what began to happen when a kid was at bat was instead of the opposing team trying to rattle him with batter-batter-batter or something similar, they yelled out words of encouragement. "Atta boy, Jack," "Great try, Dawn," "That's the way Joey." Where earlier there were exclusionary social groups, new groups evolved to encompass kids who were earlier excluded. The entire class became more bonded, happy, and kind to one another.

GUIDE TO STORY LOCATIONS

ORGANIZING THE STORIES

Classification is always challenging. For the stories in this book I've organized each into the category of best fit. Often a story can be used for more than one purpose, sometimes with tweaking. Readers will determine purposes and forums for which they might use these stories.

SHIFTING PERCEPTIONS

These stories invite listeners to move beyond current frames of reference, to entertain new ways of observing and interpreting their worlds.

INVITING LEARNING

These stories offer learning opportunities about presentation skills, courage, and internal processes.

https://youtu.be/iduMoffZ_54

Chapter 4

- Riding the Bus   perseverance in Mandarin
- ▢ The Cherokee Legend of Good Versus Evil

 https://youtu.be/TzZQm4yhPns

see what this generation hears

Chapter 5

- Fishing: A Journal Entry   we think in metaphors
- The Prince and Parables   understanding new
  ideas
- Culture Alert   mind your metaphors
- Captain Marvel   we have to be heroes

Chapter 6

- Camera Made in Japan   rapport through humor

Story Catalog

- The Alien Hand   hand with a mind of its own
- Superintendent in Shock   behaviors we don't
  understand

- ■ The Mindful Monk   gaining personal insight
- ■ Student Teacher   learning through teaching

INSPIRING ACTION

These stories inspire, encourage, and reveal how leaders influence those around them.

Chapter 1

- ■ ▢ If Women Aren't Given a Seat at the Table

 https://goo.gl/KjRBch

see brilliant storytelling

Chapter 3

- ■ One Urge at a Time   you, too, can persevere
- ■ Disliked by the Chair   observe then adapt

Chapter 4

- ■ ▢ The REAL Story of the Two Wolves

see the original good and evil story

 https://youtu.be/JHXwPFMvaXk

Chapter 7

■ ▭ Breaking Glass—A Leadership Story by Dima Ghawi at TEDxLSU

a lifetime persevering

 https://youtu.be/2nr62XUtlu0

Chapter 8

■ Bear in the Cage   enduring mental limitations

Story Catalog

■ Cramming Content   good intentions, poor results

■ Choosing a Profession   unexpected influence

■ What to Wear   given choice

■ Taking a Stand   supporting a novice teacher

SEEKING A DESIRED STATE

These stories illustrate ways presenters and leaders lead others to more productive states, attitudes, and behaviors than what currently exists.

■ Break the Pot   misdirection,
                                              then facilitation

Story Catalog
   ■ Novel Supervision Gambit   don't try this at
                                              home

APPENDIX

 Worksheet 1: Metaphor Subtexts

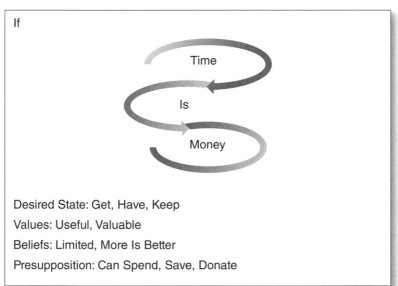

If

Time

Is

Money

Desired State: Get, Have, Keep

Values: Useful, Valuable

Beliefs: Limited, More Is Better

Presupposition: Can Spend, Save, Donate

Given the examples below, construct subtexts for the sample metaphors. Keep in mind that the subtexts drive the thinking and actions of those using the metaphor.

Metaphor:	Metaphor:	Metaphor:
Leader as Gardener	Teacher as Artist	Change as Journey
Desired State:	Desired State:	Desired State:
Values:	Values:	Values:
Beliefs:	Beliefs:	Beliefs:
Presuppositions:	Presuppositions:	Presuppositions:

Metaphor:	Metaphor:
Faculty as Team	Faculty as Family
Desired State:	Desired State:
Values:	Values:
Beliefs:	Beliefs:
Presuppositions:	Presuppositions:

Worksheet 2: Anatomy of Desired-State Stories

This worksheet series provides examples for information introduced in Chapters 8, 9, and 10 regarding the structure of desired-state stories. These stories provide a vehicle for self-correction when a group is exhibiting attitudes or behaviors that detract from their own better interests.

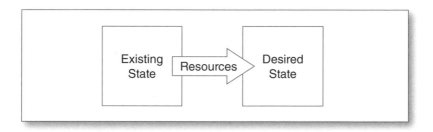

Desired-state stories employ pacing and leading, the linguistic technique presented in Chapters 8, 9, and 10. Chapter 6 introduced seven components common to well-formed stories, and Chapter 10 added four components that characterize stories for the subliminal mind. Figures from these two chapters are reintroduced here as Appendix Figure 1 and Appendix Figure 2. Worksheets 2a, 2b, and 2c give examples for the figures in the combined appendix.

Appendix Figure 1   Conditions for a Well-Formed Story

1. Factual specificity
2. Presentation congruity
3. Audience appropriate
4. Elicits empathy
5. Appropriate to workshop topic
6. Contains implicit/submerged moral
7. Creates multiple internal representations

Appendix Figure 2   Additional Conditions for a Desired-State Story

8. Bypasses protective filters
9. Parallels the audience's situation
10. Lingers on points of irresolution, internal conflicts, or discomfort
11. Marks embedded commands
12. Offers resolutions

Worksheet 2a: Evoking Internal Representations

Examples: Evoking internal representations in the Third Man Out story.

Phrases intended to evoke mental representations are in bold-face.

Good morning. I imagine some of you are thinking signing up for this program was a good idea at the time, but now you're not so sure. In any event, I hope that, like me, you have a **good summer** *behind you. This year I went backpacking in the Sierras with my buddy Ted, as I often do. But on this trip he invited another hiker, which changed everything.*

Here is what happened. Ted called. "Do you want to go to Red Can Lake this year? We could **go north** *through Yellow Hammer Canyon and then up* **to the ridge** *overlooking the lake." Excited, I said, "Sure!" Then began the process of selecting gear and arranging where to meet. We both like to travel light so I* **packed, repacked, and repacked** *some more. At the* **trailhead** *a few days later, I did a final sorting of my pack,* **hefted it to my shoulders** *(pantomiming this), and started up the initial* **climb***. I had forgotten the* **feel of the weight on my back** *and the* **torture in my legs** *going up that* **first rise***. Maybe this wasn't such a good idea after all, I thought. At the top, we sat, our* **backpacks and selves against a tree** *and* **rested***. From that point on,*

(Continued)

(Continued)

it began to be **pleasurable**. *There are always difficult spots, but getting into the* **rhythm of walking, smelling the forest aromas,** *and* **feeling** *the occasional* **cool breezes** *became* **pleasing**. *As we made it to the* **top of successive hills,** *I sometimes paused, taking in the valleys, mountains, and* **cloudless blue sky as far as the eyes could see.**

Worksheet 2b: Examples of Conditions for Well-Formed Stories

Numbers in parenthesis refer to Appendix Figure 1 and Appendix Figure 2.

THIRD MAN OUT BACKPACKING STORY

Good morning. I imagine some of you are thinking signing up for this program was a good idea at the time (8), but now you're not so sure (1) (2) (8). In any event, I hope that, like me, you have a good summer behind you. This year I went backpacking in the (1) Sierras with my buddy Ted, as I often do. But on this trip he invited another hiker, which changed everything.

Here is what happened. Ted called. "Do you want to go to Red Can Lake this year? We could go north through Yellow Hammer Canyon and then up to the ridge overlooking the lake." Excited, I said, "Sure (8)!" Then began the process of selecting gear and arranging where to meet. We both like to travel light so I packed, (1) repacked, and repacked some more. At the trailhead a few days later, I did a final sorting of my pack, hefted (7) it to my shoulders (pantomiming this), *(2) and started up the initial climb. I had forgotten the feel of the weight on my back and the torture in my legs (7)(4) going up that first rise. Maybe this wasn't such a good idea after all, I thought (8). At the top, we sat, leaned our backpacks and selves against a tree (7) and rested.*

(Continued)

(Continued)

From that point on, it began to be pleasurable (8). There are always difficult spots, but getting into the rhythm of walking, (7) smelling (7) the forest aromas, and feeling (7) the occasional cool breezes (7) became pleasing. As we made it to the top of successive hills, I sometimes paused, taking in the valleys, mountains, and cloudless blue sky (7) as far as the eyes could see.

Several days along the trail (7), Ted's friend joined us. For some reason, with him there, the trip began to lose some of its attractiveness. Sometimes I became bored (8). Sometimes I found I was irritated (7) (8) by the changed dynamics. But we trudged (7) on with no choice now to abort the trip (8). We were too far in to quit now. I found myself kicking rocks off the trail, sometimes lagging behind and throwing stones into the creeks (8) of cold, clear running water (7) that we crossed. I became disinterested (8) in the conversations even though Ted's friend had a lot of good information. Looking back, trying to figure out why I had lost interest, I had to be honest (9); Ted's friend was just boring (8). Then maybe about 140 hours into the trek, Ted's friend departed on a different trail (8).

The next rise we took opened to a better view. We were now so high, it seemed like I could actually feel the silence (7) in the still air. The soft sunlight (7) on the distant mountains gave me a sense of satisfaction (7) (10). I became aware of the play of light (7) and shadow (7) on forms around us. I also began to notice the sounds (7) of pocket gophers scurrying (7) across the granite and could hear (7) the calls of nearby birds. From this point on time seemed endless (10); we continued to trek, enjoying our surroundings (10).

Worksheet 2c: Constructing Desired Story Elements

Before using the template in Worksheet 3 to compose a story, you might like to review information about three conditions: parallel structure, lingering on points of irresolution, and embedded suggestions.

PARALLEL STRUCTURE

To develop a desired-state story, create a story that parallels the audience's situation. In Chapter 10, for example, this is done by having an "expert" interview the plants, just as the consultant had interviewed the faculty prior to the meeting in How Green Is My Garden. Another example of this is found in the Third Man Out backpacking story in Chapter 11. Some parallels in the Third Man Out story are these:

The Story	The Presenter's Assumptions About the Experience of Most Teachers
Some of you are thinking signing up for this program was a good idea at the time, but now you're not so sure.	Many teachers weigh attending a summer workshop. After the experience with the last presenter, they may be having doubts.
From that point on, it began to be pleasurable. There are always difficult spots.	The first few days of this workshop were probably fine. Problems developed only when the speaker before this presenter worked with the group.

(Continued)

(Continued)

The Story	The Presenter's Assumptions About the Experience of Most Teachers
Several days along the trail, Ted's friend joined us.	When the previous presenter did join the group.
Trying to figure out why I had lost interest, I had to be honest; Ted's friend was just boring.	Because of poor instruction, people messed around and got off track.

LINGERING ON POINTS OF IRRESOLUTION

Lingering on points of irresolution, internal conflicts, or discomfort is found in the two stories below. These are points at which listeners will go inward to search their experiences and mental models in an effort to have the story make sense to them.

How Green Is My Garden	Third Man Out
He can't quite make out what the distinction seems to be (when hearing the differences in the way plants are speaking to him).	For some reason, with him there, the trip began to lose some of its attractiveness. Sometimes I became bored. Sometimes I found I was irritated by the changed dynamics. I found myself kicking rocks off the trail.
As the expert continues to interview the plants, he gets similar data reported in these different ways. Puzzled, he ponders on the distinctions in what he is hearing.	Looking back, trying to figure out why I had lost interest, I had to be honest; Ted's friend was just boring.

EMBEDDED SUGGESTIONS

Embedded suggestions are within the story. This is another place at which listeners engage in transderivational searching. An embedded suggestion is typically located within the description of a desired state. They can also appear in other areas as shown below in underlined text.

How Green Is My Garden

"You know, I don't like it when the gardener waters, because frequently he leaves the hose unattended, water begins to flood my roots, it gets very damp and uncomfortable, <u>and I need to let him know that. So sometimes I yell, Hey, up there! Back off with the water, will ya?</u>"

Develop the story so that it bypasses defensive filters. This can be done with conversational openings as illustrated in both the gardener and backpacking stories.

How Green is My Garden	Third Man Out
Hi, I'm Bob Garmston. My job today is to give a summary of what you said in the interviews and help you start planning around whatever problems you'd like to solve. Before I start, though, I'm curious if any of you have read the new children's book *How Green is My Garden?*	Good morning. I imagine some of you are thinking signing up for this program was a good idea at the time, but now you're not so sure. In any event, I hope that, like me, you have a good summer behind you. This year I went backpacking in the Sierras.

Worksheet 3: Constructing a Desired-State Story

Step 1: Gain some understanding of the problem state and the desired state.

    a. Audience

    b. Existing state

    c. Desired state

Step 2: Create a story that is interesting to listen to and that matches the problem state and gradually moves to the desired state.

    ACTUAL SITUATION   METAPHOR

    Setting _____   becomes_____

People:

    Character 1_____   becomes_____

    Character 2_____   becomes_____

Progression of Problem

    Event 1   _____   becomes_____

    Event 2   _____   becomes_____

    Event 3   _____   becomes_____

Connecting Strategy

    Understanding of Resolution   becomes_____

Step 3:

> Write it.

> Rehearse it.

> Tell it.

POETRY REFERENCED IN THE PREFACE

In my early 80s I found myself in a hospital clinic for patients with emphysema. Trying to come to grips with the fact that my lifestyle had indeed led to this result, I wrote a poem titled *Wheezer*. The poem illustrates the challenge we sometimes face being accountable for our own behavior.

Wheezer

by Robert Garmston

not his fault

he insisted

Mt. Kilimanjaro

just one example

pushing

high altitude demands

on lungs

dripping Saudi heat

unlike Death Valley's

deathly dry air

and 4 million miles

or so

in commercial planes

oxygen in limited supply

aviation and travel to blame

particles

of certain size

affront the lungs

uncovering dry dust

and sweeping sand

summer shamals

they name the sand storms

in the Persian Gulf

and camel dung fires

trenches in the sand

place demands

on breathing apparatus

as a boy

poking his nose

into a farm barrel

of tractor fuel

thrill seeking nose

sought fumes

fueling dancing images

like drunken fireflies

frequently these highs

he later heard

collapsed alveoli

limiting oxygen

to the bronchi

sure he smoked

very cool at age 10

Camels first

like his father bought

and he with forged

notes

could get more

at the grocery store

later

stolen cartons

smokes from Safeway

became hoarded treasure

for him alone

maybe a buddy

but fault could

not be found

for his generosity

or desire to be a man

STORYTELLING
STUDY COMPANION

Robert J. Garmston and Michael Dolcemascolo

Available online

The Storytelling Study Companion is available online. The study guide offers a roadmap for a collective journey through this book. It can be accessed for free download at both the Corwin site https://us.corwin.com and the Thinking Collaborative site http://www.thinkingcollaborative.com/.

Study groups provide several benefits, including learning from diverse perspectives, enjoying a sense of commitment to the group that encourages personal preparation, and acquiring new study and storytelling skills. Additionally, study groups provide ways of examining a text deeply in relation to one's own intentions and values, deepening collegial relationships, and providing periodic opportunities for rehearsal. Generally, study groups select a study format and utilize that set of protocols throughout their period of study.

This study guide is divided into sections aligned with the *Storytelling* book chapters. Groups may decide to use the chapter guides sequentially, beginning at Chapter 1 and continuing throughout the book, or may find certain chapters immediately compelling and want to go to those first. Should you choose the latter, be aware that the study suggestions for some chapters may refer you to earlier chapters. In any event, consider this your personal resource.

It is recommended that at least one copy of *The Adaptive School: A Sourcebook for Developing Collaborative Groups, 3rd Edition* (Garmston & Wellman, 2016), is available to study groups. While this is not necessary, groups that have this *Sourcebook* can choose suggested learning activities from the extensive set of strategies on pages 197–288.

REFERENCES

Adichie, C. N. (2009, July). The danger of a single story [Video file]. Retrieved from https://www.ted.com/talks/chimamanda_adichie_the_danger_of_a_single_story

Armstrong, D. (1992). *Management by storying around: A new method of leadership*. New York, NY: Crown Business.

Austin, N., & Peters, T. (1985). *A passion for excellence: The leadership difference*. New York, NY: Grand Central.

Bandura, A. (1997). *Self-efficacy: The exercise of control*. New York, NY: Freeman.

Beavers, O. (2017). McCain: "More Shoes to Drop" on Russia Investigation. *The Hill*. Retrieved from http://thehill.com/homenews/senate/332707-mccain-trump-firing-comey-wont-stop-this-centipede-scandal

Bergen, B. (2012). *Louder than words: The new science of how the mind makes meaning*. New York, NY: Basic Books.

Bridges, W. (1980). *Transitions: Making sense of life's changes*. New York, NY: Perseus.

Bridges, W. (1991). *Managing transitions: Making the most of change*. New York, NY: Perseus.

Canfield, J., & Hansen, M. (2001). *Chicken soup for the soul*. Deerfield Beach, FL: HIC. (Original work published 1993)

Caro, R. (1990). *The passage of power: The years of Lyndon Johnson* (Vol. 4). New York, NY: Vintage.

Carpenter, A. (2015, September 17). Bridging PR and sales through storytelling [Web log]. Retrieved from https://airpr.com/blog/bridging-pr-sales-through-storytelling/

Carter-Liggett, M. (2010). *Tales for coaching: Using Stories for both individuals and small groups*. London, UK: Kogan Page Publishing.

Chen, J. (2009, November). A warm embrace that saves lives [Video file]. Retrieved from https://www.ted.com/talks/jane_chen_a_warm_embrace_that_saves_lives

Costa, A., & Garmston, R. (2016). *Cognitive coaching: Developing self-directed leaders and learners* (3rd ed.). Lanham, MD: Rowman & Littlefield.

Davis, A. (2016, March 18). How can hidden sounds be captured by everyday objects [Video file]. Retrieved from https://www.npr.org/2016/03/18/470514319/how-can-hidden-sounds-be-captured-by-everyday-objects

Delistraty, C. (2014, November 2014). The psychological comforts of storytelling. *The Atlantic*. Retrieved from https://www.theatlantic.com/health/archive/2014/11/the-psychological-comforts-of-storytelling/381964/

Denning, S. (2000). *The springboard: How storytelling ignites action in knowledge-era organizations*. Oxford, UK: Butterworth-Heinemann.

Dolan, G. (2017). *Stories for work: The essential guide to business storytelling*. Melbourne, Australia: Wiley & Sons.

Donovan, J. (2014). *How to deliver a TED Talk*. New York, NY: McGraw-Hill.

Dreazen, Y. (2015). *The invisible front: Loss and love in an era of endless war*. New York, NY: Broadway Books.

Erickson, M., & Rossi, E. (1966). *Hypnotherapy: An exploratory casebook*. New York, NY: Irvington.

Ferlatte, D. (2013, May 27). Many stories but one world [Video file]. Retrieved from https://www.youtube.com/watch?v=iduMoffZ_54

Fisher, M. (2013, October 16). The forgotten story of Iran Air flight 655 [Web log]. Retrieved from https://www.washingtonpost.com/news/worldviews/wp/2013/10/16/the-forgotten-story-of-iran-air-flight-655/?utm_term=.c3660e6c3618

Garmston, R. (2004). Anticipate change: Design a transition meeting. *Journal of Staff Development, 25*(4).

Garmston, R. (2011). *I don't do that anymore: A memoir of awakening and resilience*. Charleston, SC: CreateSpace.

Garmston, R. (2018). *The presenter's fieldbook: A practical guide* (3rd ed.). Lanham, MD: Rowman & Littlefield.

Garmston, R., & Wellman, B. (1999). *The adaptive school: A sourcebook for developing collaborative groups*. Norwood, MA: Christopher Gordon.

Garmston, R., & Wellman, B. (2017). *The adaptive school: A sourcebook for developing collaborative groups (3rd ed.)*. Lanham, MD: Rowman & Littlefield.

Garmston, R., & Zimmerman, D. (2013). *Lemons to lemonade: Resolving problems in meetings, workshops and PLCs*. Thousand Oaks, CA: Corwin.

Ghawi, D. (2014, May 15). Breaking glass: A leadership story [Video file]. Retrieved from https://www.youtube.com/watch?v=2nr62XUtlu0

Gordon, D. (2017). *Therapeutic metaphors: Helping others through the looking glass*. Independently Published. (Original work published 1978)

Grimm, J., & Grimm, W. (2011). *Grimm's complete fairy tales*. San Diego, CA: Canterbury Classics.

Grinder, J., & Bandler, R. (1975). *The structure of magic I: A book about language and therapy*. Deerfield Beach, FL: Health Communications.

Haley, J. (1993). *Uncommon therapy: The psychiatric techniques of Milton H. Erickson, M.D.* New York, NY: W.W. Norton.

Hamilton, R., & Rogerson, B. (2011) *The last storytellers: Tales from the heart of Morocco*. London, UK: I. B. Tauris.

Heath, C., & Heath, D. (2007). *Made to stick: Why some ideas survive and others die*. New York, NY: Random House.

Henley, J. (2015, December 16). Ericksons interspersal technique for pain [Web log]. Retrieved from https://www.drjameshenley.us/hypnotic-suggestions-2/ericksons-interspersal-technique-for-pain.html

Iggulden, C. (2007). *Genghis: Birth of an empire: A novel*. New York, NY: Bantam.

James, J. (1990). *The origin of consciousness in the breakdown of the bicameral mind*. New York, NY: Houghton Mifflin Harcourt. (Original work published 1976)

Jung, C. (Ed.). (1968). *Man and his symbols*. New York, NY: Random House.

Kahneman, D. (2011). *Thinking fast and slow*. New York, NY: Farrar, Straus and Giroux.

Kazantzakis, N. (2014). *Zorba the Greek*. New York, NY: Simon & Schuster.

Kerns Goodwin, D. (2006). *Teams of rivals: The political genius of Abraham Lincoln*. New York, NY: Simon & Schuster.

Kesey, K. (1997). *Sometimes a great notion*. London, UK: Penguin.

Kimmel, E. (2000). *The two mountains: An Aztec legend*. New York, NY: Holiday House.

Kusuma-Powell, O., & Powell, W. (2009). *Becoming an emotionally intelligent teacher*. Thousand Oaks, CA: Corwin.

Lakoff, G., & Johnson, M. (1980). *Metaphors we live by*. Chicago, IL: University of Chicago Press.

Landau, M., Meir, B., & Keefer, L. (2010). A metaphor-enriched social cognition. *Psychological Bulletin, 136*(6), 1045–1067.

Larson, S. (1991). *A fire in the mind: The life of Joseph Campbell*. New York, NY: Doubleday.

Lieberman, M. (2013). *Social: Why our brains are wired to connect*. New York, NY: Crown.

Malone, M. (2018, February 11). The secret to midcareer success. *Wall Street Journal*. Retrieved from https://www.wsj.com/articles/the-secret-to-midcareer-success-1518377918

Miller, A. (1976). *Death of a salesman*. New York, NY: Penguin.

Mills, J., & Crowley, R. (2014). *Therapeutic metaphors for children and the child within*. New York, NY: Routledge. (Original work published 1986)

Mock, J. (2014). *Redefining realness: My path to womanhood, identity, love & so much more*. New York, NY. Simon & Schuster.

Nelson, P. (2012). *There's a hole in my sidewalk: The romance of self-discovery*. New York, NY: Simon & Schuster.

Ness, P. (Author), & Bayona, J. A. (Director). (2016). *A monster calls* [Motion picture]. Spain: Apaches Entertainment.

O'Brien, T., & Sullivan, M. (2008). *Afghan dreams: Young voices of Afghanistan*. New York, NY: Bloomsbury.

O'Connor, J., & Seymour, J. (1990). *Introducing NLP: psychological skills for understanding and influencing people (neuro-linguistic programming)*. San Francisco, CA: Conari Press.

Palmer, A. (2013, February). The art of asking [Video file]. Retrieved from https://www.ted.com/talks/amanda_palmer_the_art_of_asking

Parkin, M. (2010). *Tales for coaching: Using stories and metaphors with individuals and small groups*. London, UK: Kogan.

Patterson, N. (2007). *Exile*. New York, NY: Henry Holt.

Patterson, R. (2017). *Alexander Hamilton: A life of inspiration*. Amazon Digital Services.

Roberts, G. (2005). *Shantaram: A novel*. New York, NY: St. Martin's.

Rosen, S. (1982). *My voice will go with you: Teaching tales of Milton Erickson*. New York, NY: Norton.

Sacks, O. (1998). *The man who mistook his wife for a hat: And other clinical tales.* New York, NY: Touchstone.

Sartore, R. (1994). *Joseph Campbell on myth and mythology.* Chicago, IL: University Press of America.

Satrapi, M. (2004). *Persepolis: The story of a childhood.* New York, NY: Pantheon.

Schaef, A. W. (1995). *Native wisdom for white minds: Daily reflections inspired by the native peoples of the world.* New York, NY: One World.

Shakespeare, W. (2017). *Hamlet.* Seattle, WA: Amazon Classics.

Smith, A. (2016). *Danger close: My epic journey as a combat helicopter pilot in Iraq and Afghanistan.* New York, NY: Simon & Shuster.

Stone, I. (1956). *Men to match my mountains.* New York, NY: Berkley Press.

Swanson, L., Newman, E., Araque, A., & Dubinsky, J. (2017). *The beautiful brain: The drawings of Santiago* (Kindle ed.). New York, NY: Abrams.

Thibodeau, P. (2017, August 31). "Blow the whistle" or "Stop the leaks?" *Behavioral Scientist.* Retrieved from http://behavioralscientist.org/blow-whistle-stop-leaks/

Thor, B. (2017). *Use of force: A thriller.* New York, NY: Simon & Schuster.

Wagler, I. (2011). *Growing up Amish: A memoir.* Hillsboro, OR: Tyndale House.

Wiessner, P. W. (2014). Embers of society: Firelight talk among the Ju/'hoansi Bushmen. *Proceedings of the National Academy of Science, 111*(39), 14027–14035. Retrieved from https://doi.org/10.1073/pnas.1404212111

Wilson, M. (1957). But he doesn't know the territory. [The Music Man, film version 1962]. Adapted from *Rock Island.*

Zak, P. (2014). Why your brain loves good storytelling. *Harvard Business Review.* Retrieved from https://hbr.org/2014/10/why-your-brain-loves-good-storytelling

Zoller, K. (2012, December 13). 3rd point (pre-assessment video): The choreography of presenting Kendall Zoller and Claudette Laundry [Video File]. Retrieved from https://www.youtube.com/watch?v=2NyXbd6r7mI

Zoller, K., & Landry, C. (2010). *The choreography of presenting: The 7 essential abilities of effective presenters.* Thousand Oaks, CA: Corwin.

Zumbach, L. (2016, October 25). United's Newest Crew Member: Chief Storyteller. *Chicago Tribune.*

INDEX

CORWIN
LEADERSHIP

Anthony Kim & Alexis Gonzales-Black
Designed to foster flexibility and continuous innovation, this resource expands cutting-edge management and organizational techniques to empower schools with the agility and responsiveness vital to their new environment.

Jonathan Eckert
Explore the collective and reflective approach to progress, process, and programs that will build conditions that lead to strong leadership and teaching, which will improve student outcomes.

PJ Caposey
Offering a fresh perspective on teacher evaluation, this book guides administrators to transform their school culture and evaluation process to improve teacher practice and, ultimately, student achievement.

Dwight L. Carter & Mark White
Through understanding the past and envisioning the future, the authors use practical exercises and real-life examples to draw the blueprint for adapting schools to the age of hyper-change.

Raymond L. Smith & Julie R. Smith
This solid, sustainable, and laser-sharp focus on instructional leadership strategies for coaching might just be your most impactful investment toward student achievement.

Simon T. Bailey & Marceta F. Reilly
This engaging resource provides a simple, sustainable framework that will help you move your school from mediocrity to brilliance.

Debbie Silver & Dedra Stafford
Equip educators to develop resilient and mindful learners primed for academic growth and personal success.

Peter Gamwell & Jane Daly
Discover a new perspective on how to nurture creativity, innovation, leadership, and engagement.

Leadership That Makes an Impact

Steven Katz, Lisa Ain Dack, & John Malloy

Leverage the oppositional forces of top-down expectations and bottom-up experience to create an intelligent, responsive school.

Peter M. DeWitt

Centered on staff efficacy, these resources present discussion questions, vignettes, strategies, and action steps to improve school climate, leadership collaboration, and student growth.

Eric Sheninger

Harness digital resources to create a new school culture, increase communication and student engagement, facilitate real-time professional growth, and access new opportunities for your school.

Russell J. Quaglia, Kristine Fox, Deborah Young, Michael J. Corso, & Lisa L. Lande

Listen to your school's voice to see how you can increase engagement, involvement, and academic motivation.

Michael Fullan, Joanne Quinn, & Joanne McEachen

Learn the right drivers to mobilize complex, coherent, whole-system change and transform learning for all students.

CORWIN LEADERSHIP

A SAGE Publishing Company

CORWIN HAS ONE MISSION: to enhance education through intentional professional learning.

We build long-term relationships with our authors, educators, clients, and associations who partner with us to develop and continuously improve the best evidence-based practices that establish and support lifelong learning.